THE JOURNEY
TO THE INNER CHAMBER

Discovering the Treasure of the Universe

The book you are about to read is an allegory.
An allegory conveys deeper truths within the framework
of the story. In other words, it is a story within a story.
Although the characters and events you will read about are
fictitious, they are drawn from personal experiences I have
had, and based on people I have known. To these unsung
heroes of the faith, and people like them, I dedicate this book.

Rocky Fleming — February 2010

THE JOURNEY
TO THE INNER CHAMBER

Discovering the Treasure of the Universe

ROCKY FLEMING

Published by Prayer Cottage Publications
Bella Vista, Arkansas

Scripture taken from the New American Standard Bible,®
Copyright ©The Lockman Foundation.

Printed in the United States of America

Cover Photo:
The Whirlpool Galaxy from the Hubble Telescope
NASA, ESA, S. Beckwith (STScI),
and The Hubble Heritage Team (STScI/AURA)

Book design by Lorinda Gray/The Ragamuffin Acre

ISBN 0-9742383-1-7

Table of Contents

PART ONE

PART TWO

PART ONE

Chapter 1

The Wake-Up Call

I WAS HAVING ANOTHER FITFUL NIGHT'S SLEEP. It could have been the winter storm blowing outside that woke me up. I doubt it, though, for I had been waking up often for several weeks. It was taking its toll. You see, I'm a businessman who usually puts in a stressful day's work, and I need my sleep. But it was getting to the point that I couldn't put in a good day's work; I was always tired. My family tiptoed around like I was a wounded dog ready to bite anyone who came near. I don't think anyone liked me then. Heck, I didn't even like myself.

I decided to get up. It was 3 a.m. There's not much you can do at that time of night. If you get up and stay up, the fatigue hits you like a ton of bricks at about noon. If you stay in bed and struggle to go back to sleep, you eventually get only about an hour's nap and you feel terrible all day. It was getting to be a regular sleep cycle, and it was getting to me.

I had heard a friend say he was having some problems like that and decided to use the time for prayer. He felt that either the devil was waking him up or the Lord was. If it were the devil waking him, he would make him regret it by praising the Lord. If it was the Lord waking him, it must be for a good reason and he wanted to get up and listen to what the Lord wanted to say. I didn't know what or who was waking me, but I thought the prayer idea was a good one. So I went to the study, got a blanket, wrapped myself in it and lay prostrate on the floor.

The house was quiet as the children and my wife slept soundly. The storm was still kicking up. The wind made an eerie sound as it whistled through the trees and around the house.

"Lord," I prayed, "I don't know what's going on. It might be the sleep disruption that's getting to me, but I think something else has been disturbing me for quite a while. Will You help me see what it is?" Not really expecting an answer I lay quietly on the floor and attempted to find some sort of sleep.

It was in that nether world of being awake or being asleep I heard the words: "Stop resisting Me and come to the Feast in the Inner Chamber."

3

I was shocked and now wide-awake. I rose up from my position on the floor and looked around to see if anyone was in the room. Not seeing anyone and not knowing what to make of it, I settled back to my former position. As I settled down again and began to listen to the storm outside the house, I felt a deep impression that can only be described as "an inner voice" that seemed like a whisper. "Come to My Inner Chamber," was whispered again.

By this time I realized that something new and spectacular was breaking through my self-made, pragmatic personality. I knew that I must go with the flow and respond to what was being impressed into my mind and heart. I audibly replied, "Lord, how am I resisting You?"

A whisper answered me, "You are trying to remain the old person, and I want to make you a new man." "What must I do to let You make me the man You want me to be?" I responded.

"You must let go of trying to keep control of your life and partake of the Feast in the Inner Chamber."

With fear and excitement pumping my heart, I understood that the Lord was about to show me something fresh and new about Himself. I had been learning to trust Him more and more, but not without the difficulty of abandoning my own way of doing things. This was one of those times I would have to let go of my pragmatic reasoning and let Him take me on the journey He wanted to take me on.

"Savior," I prayed, "I want to be the man You want to make me. I ask You to show me the Feast in the Inner Chamber so that I can partake of it."

Now, I'm new at this. I'm not sure how a vision works, so all I can do is describe what happened. When I asked my Savior to show me where the Feast in the Inner Chamber was, the room around me began to fade. The more the room faded, the clearer a new scene became. At first it was hard to see because a fog engulfed me. When things began to clear, I could see that I had been in a cloudbank and was now being gently lowered to earth. As I was lowered, I saw a beautiful green valley with a flowing stream. In the center of the valley was a medieval castle, complete with mote and drawbridge. In the fields surrounding the castle were tents and thousands of people walking aimlessly. I also saw a small flow of people making their way toward the castle. The scene intrigued me. "Lord," I asked, "What am I seeing here? Where is this place, and who are those people?"

"Be patient," He replied, "for I am about to allow you to see a vision that involves the spiritual progression to maturity with one of My children. When this vision is complete, you will understand what you are to do to become the man I want you to be."

He continued, "I am giving to you a guide whose name is Messenger. You may ask him at any point to help you understand what you are seeing, and he will explain what it means."

Chapter 2

The Refugee Camp

WHEN I GENTLY TOUCHED DOWN, I was in the midst of the people surrounding the castle. I immediately realized that I could see them, but they could not see me. I saw that something was deathly wrong. All of the people looked as if they were at the point of death. Their eyes were sunken into their skulls. Their rib cages showed. They walked about aimlessly. Once in a while I would see one of the walking skeletons collapse, dead. When it happened, men in long black robes would load the body into a cart and cast it into a fire. It was the most horrific thing I had ever seen.

As I looked, I heard a voice say, "It's a troubling scene, is it not?"

I turned and saw a man unlike any I had ever seen. He was tall and muscular and had piercing eyes that would have intimidated me except for the look of kindness and compassion that softened his stare. By his wardrobe and aura, I could tell he was angelic. From the sword and the combat scars on his body, I concluded that he was a mighty warrior who had seen many battles. He had the look of one in command, but also one who had seen hand-to-hand combat. I had heard that when one sees real moral authority and authenticity, no further introduction is needed. I was seeing the real thing, and I knew it. He had my attention.

"I am Messenger. I will guide you through this vision," the man said. "Ask whatever you wish, and I will make clear its meaning."

"What am I seeing here?" I asked.

"The castle represents the Lord's Kingdom that has been established in your world. The grounds outside the castle represent the temporary dwelling place for the people of your world. The people and their condition represent mankind. What you are seeing in these pitiful individuals is the true inner condition of the hearts and souls of mankind. That is why they look as if they are starving.

"Many people in your world do not appear that way because of the mask of man-made success and prosperity. However, deep in their inner being it is true, and it is only a matter of time before they know it. You see mankind is starving for a relationship with his Creator. Unless he finds it he will surely perish. Unless he comes into the Kingdom and eats from God's table, he will surely die," Messenger concluded.

"Messenger," I asked, "What caused this starving condition in mankind?"

He answered, "Because the father and mother of mankind chose to disobey the Creator while in the paradise He created for them, the process of spiritual starvation began. The sin of mankind's parents created a separation from the Creator, for themselves and all their children. However, in His mercy and grace, God created a way for mankind to come back to Him. It is the only solution for mankind's redemption and survival. That solution, and it alone, brings mankind back to the Creator."

"Sir," I asked with exasperation, "Why don't they just go back to God? All they have to do is look around and see the condition they are in."

"The great Deceiver convinces them that there is no problem his remedies can't fix. He dulls them with earthly treasures. He makes them feel special by appealing to their pride. He appears as an angel of light and convinces them that all they need is what he offers. A little more money or a new job or a new love in their life or the applause of man—these are some of his misleading strategies. But what he is really doing is leading them to the fire that will eventually consume them along with him. Think of your world, and you will remember the counterfeits that keep people from seeing the truth and trusting God's provision. Think of your own life and the counterfeits you had to overcome."

I thought of my own struggle with faith in God and how I resisted Him for so long. I once thought fame and fortune were all I needed. Because I had come from a background where money was tight, I thought that all I needed for happiness was plenty of money, a beautiful wife, children and things to entertain me. Therefore, I worked hard and put in a lot of time and effort in my career. Eventually I began to see some things come through for me. I began to realize my dream of financial success. But by that point, my family was close to breaking up and all I really cared for was about to leave me.

My family and my life, for that matter, would have been ruined had it not been for a friend who showed me what it meant to be a true believer. That friend didn't say much. He just served me and loved me, but best of all he was authentic. He just lived it out. He had no title or degree or the riches of the world. But his joy and his perspective of life were so beautiful and appealing that it made me want it. I could see by his life and his pursuit of Christ that he had the answers. I began to realize that I had been deceived in thinking that gaining the world's riches at the price of my soul and my family was a fair trade. Fair trade? It would be the trade of a fool! That friend helped me see the truth by leading me to Christ and to freedom. When Christ came into my life, He changed my world, especially my marriage. He brought healing and health back to it. He helped me get my priorities straight. I thought I had been progressing nicely, but I was now aware that something was still missing and the Father was about to show me what it was.

After remembering those things I answered Messenger, "Yes, I remember the counterfeits now."

As I began to scan the starving crowd, I saw something that was in stark contrast to the misery I had been viewing. Riding through the crowd, mounted on magnificent horses, were riders dressed in gleaming armor. The armor, the noble steeds and the riders' air of confidence were handsome and appealing. As I watched the riders move gently through the crowds, I saw flaming arrows being shot at them from hideous creatures that were walking through the crowd of humans. The flaming missiles had no effect, though, as they bounced off the riders' armor and shields. As I contemplated what I was seeing, Messenger said, "Now, watch what happens, for you will start to understand the man whom God wants you to become and what must happen for you to become that man."

Chapter 3

Influence to Refugee

ONE OF THE RIDERS DISMOUNTED and went directly to a starving human who was slumped near me. The rider said something I couldn't hear. The starving man nodded weakly. Then the rider removed a flask of water that had been strapped to his side. He gently lifted the man's head and let him drink. Next the rider opened a bag and took fruit and bread from it. He again assisted the starving human by lifting his head while he ate. All the while the rider stroked the human's back and offered comfort. The human gained enough strength from the nourishment to stand. At this point the rider lifted the once starving man to the back of his noble steed and mounted it with him. The rider held his shield over the human to protect him from the flaming arrows. As they rode toward the castle, the rider continued to share his food and water with the human as he protected him from the arrows.

"Messenger," I asked excitedly, "who are those two people, and what have I just seen?"

He replied, "The starving man is called Refugee, for he lives in a country that is not his own. Refugee is the inner man of someone in your world with whom you are familiar. The rider is called Influencer."

I certainly couldn't see any familiarity in the person I was looking at in Refugee, so I decided to ask more about him later. I was more intrigued by the other person, so I asked:

"Who is Influencer?"

"He is one of the warriors the Lord has dispatched from the Feast in the Inner Chamber. His work for the Father is to influence humans like Refugee to come to our King's castle. Influencer uses his unique talents and gifts as he serves the human. With the King of Kings' Spirit within him, coupled with his own special ways, Influencer becomes the Lord's voice, His hands and His ministry to mankind."

"You have just seen Influencer reach out to Refugee and serve him at his basic point of need. He shared with Refugee the food and water he had received himself

11

from his time in the Inner Chamber. The food and water taken from this feast and shared in the Lord's name with a needy person can have a powerful impact on mankind as you just saw."

Messenger continued, "Did you notice the gentle rubbing of Refugee's back while Influencer ministered to his needs? This is the symbolic act of a powerful but gentle warrior, who does not condemn or judge the human, for Influencer knows firsthand the struggles that Refugee is going through. He knows Refugee needs more than food and water, that he needs unconditional acceptance. Influencer's work is always to point a human back to his King, and he cannot do this if he is arrogant and judgmental. He is careful in how he helps Refugee so that this doesn't happen. He maintains a humble attitude and shows respect for the human. Influencer also knows that Refugee needs to see God's love in action. This makes Refugee want to take the next step toward the Father and His kingdom."

"What about those hideous creatures that are shooting flaming arrows at Influencer?" I asked.

Messenger answered, "They are soldiers of the great Deceiver, the enemy of the Lord and mankind. These creatures are doing their best to keep the humans in their miserable condition. They don't want the humans to be saved from the ultimate death and fire they will face. By shooting at Influencer, they are trying to wound or discourage him. But their arrows cannot get to him. As long as Influencer keeps partaking of the Feast in the Inner Chamber, he will be strong and resist their arrows. The armor that Influencer wears will stand against the flaming missiles and all other schemes of the Deceiver."

"Influencer is filled with the Lord's Spirit because he comes directly from the Feast in the Inner Chamber," he continued. "He can discern which humans' hearts are ready to receive his help. Unless one is filled with the Lord's Spirit, he cannot understand what I am saying. But Influencer understands, for he partakes regularly at the feast, and this makes him sensitive to Refugee's heart. Watch what happens as Influencer takes Refugee toward the King's castle."

Chapter 4

To The Kingdom

I FOLLOWED INFLUENCER AND REFUGEE toward the castle. I noticed that other riders had placed starving humans on their horses and were headed for the castle, as well.

As we moved forward, I noticed a throng of starving humans eating at tables outside the castle walls. Influencer paid no attention to the activity, but I noticed that Refugee was looking longingly at the food that was being passed out. Refugee began to point to the food and motioned to Influencer that he wanted to go to it. I saw Influencer stop, turn to Refugee and speak to him while motioning to the food. After a moment, Refugee nodded as if he understood what Influencer was saying, and they continued their journey. I had to ask, for I couldn't understand why Influencer wouldn't let Refugee eat when food was obviously available.

"Look closely at what is being offered. Also look at the results. You will see one of the great deceptions that the Deceiver gives to mankind," he responded.

I eased through the crowd and looked at the food. There was nothing of substance. It looked like many of the appetizers I had seen at parties. They were fun, interesting and different looking but lacked nutritional value. I looked closely at the people who were fighting for the dainty items. I wanted to see whether the appetizers made any difference, but I saw no change in their starving appearance. They were still the same pitiful-looking wretches who were destined for death and fire. They were still dying of malnutrition. But most of them had lost their hunger pangs and their raging appetites had abated. Again, I needed to ask the meaning of what I saw.

"What is being offered has no substance and the starving humans are not saved from their destiny of death and fire. Can you tell me what else this means?" I asked.

"Think of your world," Messenger answered. "What you are seeing is a representation of one of the great deceptions of your age. The great Deceiver has established different religions for mankind that are designed to take away mankind's hunger for the Father. The appetizers represent these religions. The Deceiver knows that mankind is starving for a restored relationship with the Lord. Therefore, he has created counterfeits that will divert the people by giving them a false enlightenment. They think that when they partake of these religions they know Him and have a right relationship with Him, but they have been led astray. I call these humans Religion Victims."

Messenger continued, "A Religion Victim is a seeker who is looking and sampling on the periphery of knowing God. These people try a lot of religions in hopes of finding Him. They try everything from legalism to Buddhism. They try Eastern Mysticism to Transcendentalism. You name the 'ism,' and they try it. They just won't take the simple truth of God's provision, which allows them to come to Him, for they are deceived in thinking there is, something else. I tell you, any pursuit of God that does not come through His provision alone will not find Him. There is only one path to God and that is through His Son, Jesus Christ."

"What is most distressing is that there are some churches in this group that are called by Jesus' name. But they teach that there are other ways to God and that Jesus is only one of many. I tell you, teachers of this false doctrine will be dealt with most severely on Judgment Day. Know this: Jesus Christ, God's only provision for mankind, will never be found in the appetizer section with other religions."

Messenger continued. "Christianity should never be identified as a religion, for what is offered is a right relationship with God through His grace. It is not a result of mankind's works or religious behavior. I detest it when people call God's provision 'religion'!"

I thought Messenger was finished, but it was obvious that he was highly agitated over the religion thing. So he continued.

"What do religions bring that is so appetizing? Legalistic rules that give a false sense of security? Programs that attempt to box God in by trying to make Him something they can understand, rather than considering that He is unimaginable and inestimable? What about the self-actualization religions? All they do is feed their ego needs. Make no mistake: To a hungry person these 'appetizer religions' look good and do what the Deceiver designed them to do. They will keep people from the real thing, the real feast that is found in a personal, intimate relationship with God through His Son, Jesus Christ and they must be avoided."

"I understand," was my simple reply.

Chapter 5

The Bridge to the Kingdom

BY THIS TIME INFLUENCER AND REFUGEE had gone on, so I rushed to catch up. When I had caught up with them, Influencer had already helped Refugee off his horse. They were talking intently. Influencer was motioning toward the drawbridge that crossed the mote. I noticed that the bridge was up. As I watched them, Influencer stopped talking. He and Refugee embraced, and Influencer backed away and closely watched Refugee. Next I watched Refugee fall to his knees, clasp his hands under his chin and start to pray. I couldn't hear his prayer, but as he was praying, the drawbridge began to be lowered slowly. When Refugee opened his eyes and saw the drawbridge down before him, an indescribable smile crossed his face. Influencer was beaming. It looked as if the relationship of Influencer and Refugee changed before my eyes. I was no longer seeing strangers who had become friends and were embracing each other. I was now seeing brothers who had been estranged but were back together. Both Influencer and Refugee were weeping. But these were not the tears of pain or heartbreak. They were tears of unspeakable joy.

After a brief celebration, Influencer and Refugee crossed the drawbridge arm in arm and proceeded into the castle.

"Oh, sir, what have I seen here?" I asked. "This is the most touching scene I have ever seen."

Messenger answered, "You have just seen the birth of a new child to God's kingdom. Refugee has crossed the Bridge and is now in God's family."

He continued, "Remember, what you are seeing relates to your world under its surface view. As you know, the castle represents God's Kingdom in your world. The grounds outside the castle represent the world you live in. The people outside His castle are starving and deceived refugees who are bound for death and fire unless they eat at the Lord's table. Around the Kingdom of God is an unconquerable moat that mankind can't cross. The moat represents the great separation that occurred when sin came into mankind. God is holy and mankind is sinful. Holiness and sin cannot exist together, and the separation exists because of this."

"The great Deceiver has much of mankind convinced that good works and religion can cross the moat and scale the walls to God's kingdom. They cannot. There is no good work that mankind can do, nor any religion that can conquer this separation. There is only one way to enter His Kingdom and that is over the Bridge that God established. The Bridge that Refugee just crossed represents God's provision for mankind, which is His Son, Jesus Christ. He is the way, the truth and the life, and no one can come to God in any other way. Mankind must come through Him alone. Jesus is the Bridge from God to mankind. Jesus laid down His life for mankind in obedience to the Father so that whoever would believe this and come to God through this belief would be saved from death and fire."

"The decision to cross the Bridge had to be made by Refugee alone. Influencer had explained the process to Refugee. He walked Refugee all the way to a point of decision, but it was Refugee's choice to make. Coming to God cannot be attained through parents, friends or well-wishers. A person may grow up in church and have a family legacy of belief in Jesus, but the decision is still up to him. The Father has no grandchildren, only children. This is the reason you saw Influencer step away from Refugee when the time came for the decision. It was between Refugee and God."

"Refugee recognized the gift that was being offered to him through God's provision. Influencer had done a good job, by his life's example, of getting the point across to Refugee. But the decision was now in Refugee's hands, and he made his decision. When Refugee prayed to the Lord, he said he recognized that he was a sinner and was lost. He said he was aware that he didn't deserve His love or the salvation that was being offered. He was tired of the life he was living and wanted to give it to God to do with as He saw fit. Refugee said he wanted to receive the provision that had been made for him and become God's child. At that point, the Bridge was lowered and you saw what happened."

I was amazed at this explanation. As tears of joy fell from my cheeks, I couldn't help but remember the time I prayed that prayer and crossed the Bridge to the Father. I was reminded of the joy of my salvation and how I had promised myself that I would never forget what I had been saved from. I also remembered the influencer that God dispatched to me and how that man explained to me how to get to the Bridge.

In this vision, I had been led into a hidden world that represented to me the inner condition of mankind and the battles that are going on behind the scenes and out of sight. At first I was having a hard time grasping an understanding of what I was seeing. However, as my view was adjusted and I began to look with spiritual eyes and understand those things that are not seen by the flesh, it had become crystal clear why it had been represented to me as it had. We are spiritual beings that live temporarily in a body of flesh. Although we think our life battles are fought in the flesh and with others of the flesh, our greatest battles are being waged in this inner world that I had been brought to. The battles being waged here are for the soul of man. It is the soul that lives after the flesh dies and it is a matter of where that soul resides for eternity. This world and the battles being waged here are beyond any description as to their importance. For the first time I was frightened by what was going on in the spiritual world and my lack of involvement in the rescue of other refugees outside the Kingdom. I was also concerned about the danger I could be in and was oblivious to. I was anxious to continue following Influencer and Refugee as they continued their journey.

Chapter 6

The Outer Courtyard

AFTER MY THOUGHTS, I followed Influencer and Refugee over the drawbridge and into the outer courtyard of the castle. As Refugee crossed the Bridge, a miraculous transformation occurred. A gleaming white robe replaced the old dirty clothes that Refugee had been wearing. I saw Influencer whisper something to Refugee. I asked Messenger what had been said and the meaning of the new garments.

He replied, "When Refugee crossed over the Bridge and into God's Kingdom, two things happened. First, all his sins were forgiven. The gleaming white robe that replaced his old filthy garments is symbolic of being washed by the blood of the Lamb. This means all of his past sins were removed from God's sight and memory. Next, Influencer whispered these words to Refugee. Listen to what he said."

Almost as if I was hearing a taped replay, I heard Influencer say to Refugee in his own voice: "You once were lost, but now you have been found. You once were blind, but now you see. You once were filthy with sin, but now you are clean. You once were a wandering vagabond with no country of your own, but now you are a citizen of God's Kingdom. You once were an orphan, but now you are a child of the King of Kings. You once were called Refugee, but that name has been changed just like you have been changed. Your new name is Learner."

As I heard Influencer's words, I remembered that being given a fresh start with Christ was one of the great joys of having my sins forgiven. I remembered how the influencer in my life had helped me see myself differently. He was always reinforcing my decision to trust Jesus by reminding me when life got tough, that He who loved me beyond imagination was with me. In the early days after my decision, it was important that this follow-up take place, for I was still weak and childish. I see that this is what Influencer was doing with Refugee, now called Learner.

I began to look around the courtyard. We were not yet in the castle but were within the Kingdom of God. As Influencer and Learner walked arm in arm toward the castle, I noticed a scene similar to what had occurred outside. There were tables with food. Standing around the tables were former refugees in their gleaming white robes. They were eating something, but I noticed that the refugees had changed only slightly in appearance. Although they didn't look like walking death anymore, they still looked frail, sickly and vulnerable to disease. Learner said something to Influencer. I could tell that Learner wanted to dig into what was being offered, but Influencer stopped and explained something. Learner nodded, and he and Influencer kept moving toward the castle.

I asked, "Messenger, what I am seeing here? Why couldn't Learner eat at this place?"

Messenger responded, "You have seen Learner come across the Bridge and enter into a relationship with God. He did that when he accepted God's provision. But he still has a long way to go before he is the mature spiritual man he needs to be. The maturity I speak of requires real spiritual food. Influencer explained this to him and told him that this is not the place to stop if he wants to mature and become spiritually healthy. You will note that other former refugees stopped to eat. Look at what they are eating and you will understand better why they are not getting as healthy as they should."

I moved toward the table, which was full of various kinds of sweets. They were attractive and tasty but offered little nutrition. It was little wonder that the refugees eating here were not getting stronger and still looked frail.

"What does this represent?" I asked.

Messenger replied, "In your world, some churches have forgotten their mission to feed the flocks that have been entrusted to them, with the real food found in God's Word. This food and the table represent those particular churches.

"Those churches have diluted God's Word to make it acceptable to their congregations. For the most part, they have good hearts and intentions, but their message is laced with a worldly agenda and they no longer teach the total truth that was given to them for building up the Church. They have sweetened their message and watered it down to make it attractive and easily digested by the babies in their congregation. In doing so they are creating confusion and a mixed message. This is why many in their congregation think that right is wrong and wrong is right. These teachers don't want to offend but consequently they allow their flocks to wallow in ignorance and unrepentance. They offer an explanation that God's grace covers it all but the real reason they say this is because they are afraid to speak a truth that will divide the congregation."

"If they speak God's Word in total and in truth, it will divide darkness from light. But, if they do, God's children will grow strong and be made safe. If these churches do not speak the truth of God's Word and let it work its way into His children's hearts, these children will stay spiritually anemic and be susceptible to the flaming arrows in their everyday lives. A steady diet of sweet messages is the wrong diet for God's children, for this kind of food is not nutritious enough to grow them into mature believers."

After Messenger completed his explanation, he instructed me to follow Learner and Influencer into the castle.

Chapter 7

The Banquet Table

I ASCENDED THE CASTLE STAIRS, walked through massive doors and entered a large banquet hall. As I surveyed the room, I noticed a long table in the center of the hall. Around the table stood several people. It was apparent that these people were strategically placed to assist those who ate at the table. They seemed poised and ready to serve.

The large table held foods that progressed from baby food at one end to heartier, meatier foods at the other. The type of food grew progressively more solid and nutritious.

At the end of table where the heartier foods were placed, an extensive variety was available. There was no baby food to be found in this area, only meats, vegetables and fruits of the most exotic variety.

As I watched Learner and Influencer enter the banquet hall, Influencer introduced Learner to another individual who stood at the table. This person looked mature and had an aura of confidence much like Influencer but with characteristics unique to him. After the introduction, Influencer stepped aside while the other individual put his arm around Learner. This new character stepped toward the table with Learner. Learner was then seated at the end of the table with the baby foods. The new individual prayed with Learner first and began to spoon-feed him as a mother would a baby. By this time I was ready to explode with questions, so I asked Messenger to explain what I had seen.

"What you have seen so far and will see more later," he answered, "is a representation in your world of how the Father spiritually matures His children. The food in this banquet hall represents God's Word. Learner will be fed easily digestible food at first, and when he is able, he will be moved to more substantial food. Likewise in your world, the new child of God needs to be spoon-fed God's Word initially with the simple basics of the gospel. As the new baby in Christ matures, he needs to be moved to a deeper understanding of God's truths that are hidden in the Bible. Understand this: God's Word is carefully inspired by Him and is given to His children for understanding the life He wants you to live, to inspire you, to correct you when there is wrong behavior and to draw you into a closer communion with Him. Simply put, His Word will teach you how to live the life that His child should live."

Messenger continued, "Because Learner is new to God's Kingdom and has been without food, he needs help with his diet. He needs to be fed like a baby, for he will have a hard time understanding his special dietary needs. He has to be fed by someone equipped to understand those special needs. For this reason you have seen Influencer introduce Learner to someone who can minister to his needs. That person's name is Mentor.

"Mentor is specially gifted by the Father for this work. He knows how to nurture a new baby like Learner. He will spoon feed him the baby food, and when Learner is ready, Mentor will begin to introduce stronger food into his diet. Mentor will move Learner progressively toward the other end of the table, where he will feed him with the meatier foods.

"Did you notice that Mentor prayed with Learner before the meal?" Messenger asked. "Prayer is equally essential in the diet of the believer. Mentor is modeling the way a believer learns to communicate with God. In prayer a believer speaks to God. In His Word, God communicates to the believer. In the early stages of a believer's relationship with God, the intake of God's Word and prayer are often segmented. But in the maturing process the segments begin to merge and real communication with God and the believer are enjoyed. Simply put, the believer learns to speak and listen in a balanced manner, as one would do with his best friend. This will be an important part of Mentor's guidance with Learner's maturing process."

I understood the dynamics better now that Messenger had explained it to me. I could see the wonderful benefit of having a specialist working with Learner and how that would be ideal in my world, as someone would carefully nurture a new believer who knew his special needs. But I still had questions about Influencer and the other people I was seeing around the banquet table. So I asked:

"I have a question about Influencer. Wouldn't it be Influencer's duty to feed Learner, since he is the one who was with him the whole journey?"

"Not necessarily," Messenger replied. "In some cases Influencer could be that person. However, it depends on several factors, including some special needs that Learner has that Influencer might not be equipped to handle. Let me give you a clearer picture of God's design so you will better understand the beauty of God's plan.

"As I said before, in this banquet hall you see a representation of the progress of a new believer in your world as he grows from childhood to spiritual maturity.

God has designed His Church to be highly coordinated in this effort. Each believer plays an important part in growing His children to spiritual maturity. Each believer is given magnificent gifts of the Spirit so that he can participate in this plan and help build the Church. Mentor is representative of the gifted teachers God has placed in the Church. Examples of Mentor are seen in pastors, small-group leaders, campus ministers and youth leaders. You will find the gift of teaching at work in many places. It and all the other gifts play a vital role in a believer's spiritual maturity."

Messenger paused so that I could comprehend what he had just said.

"Now, to your question about Influencer," Messenger began. "Influencer's gifts and strategic placement by God are best used in the world outside the castle. In your world he represents a believer who is a typical businessman, professional, laborer, teacher, student or retiree. He has no pulpit, no credentials, no title or anything to distinguish him from the people around him. He draws no attention to himself but deflects all attention to his King. He could be viewed as God's secret agent. The thing that Influencer does best is representing God to the world by his character, his integrity and his countenance. Of course, his own spiritual gifts come into play in how he influences the people around him. But, simply put, Influencer is a champion of his King's cause. For this reason, he not only has to wear the armor for warfare and be ready to stand firm against the enemy as he serves in the marketplace, he also must be a gentle warrior and represent God's characteristics to the people around him."

Messenger continued, "The other people you see are influencers in their own way. They represent the Spirit-gifted people who serve God's cause in many other places, such as the home, hospitals and prisons. But these people influence differently from how Influencer works because of how they are gifted and where God places them.

"I want you to watch Mentor work with Learner. You will better understand Learner's needs and God's plan when you go to the Feast in the Inner Chamber."

I was surprised to hear Messenger say the Feast in the Inner Chamber was still ahead. I thought I had been seeing the Feast. All the food and service made available for Learner were beyond anything I could compare it with. I didn't see how anything could be better than this. I thought, "If this isn't the Feast that I am being led to, I can't imagine how grand and spectacular it must be."

I was beginning to understand that there is a process necessary for preparing Learner and the believer for the Feast. I also began to realize that this progression was being shown to me so that I could understand what was missing in my own life and what was keeping me from the Feast in the Inner Chamber.

Chapter 8

Making New Muscles

I HEEDED MESSENGER'S INSTRUCTION to watch Mentor and Learner. After one of Learner's meals, I saw Mentor instruct him to leave the table and go to a room off the banquet hall. I followed.

The room that Learner and Mentor entered was a large exercise room. It had all of the weights and equipment that could be found in the finest gyms. Mentor had Learner working on some light weights. Then he led Learner to a cot and instructed him to rest. After a while, Mentor took Learner back to the table to pray and be fed. He moved Learner closer to the heavier foods. After Learner ate, the cycle of training and resting would be repeated. Each time Learner entered the exercise room, greater weights were added to Learner's training regimen. This seemed confusing; if it related to spiritual growth in my world, I needed Messenger to clear it up. I asked that he help me understand the scene.

"You were at one time an athlete in your world, were you not?" He asked.

I nodded, "Yes."

Messenger continued, "Well, think about your training. Were there not three main components for getting stronger and physically mature: nutrition, exercise and rest? What would it have been like if you participated in only one or two of the three? Nutrition without exercise would lead to fat. Rest without exercise would lead to laziness. Exercise without nutrition and rest would lead to physical breakdown. It is the same with spiritual growth.

"Again, I say, you are seeing a representation here in order to hammer home truth as it relates to a believer's spiritual growth in your world, so listen carefully."

I was all ears.

"The food in the banquet hall represents the nutritional value of God's Word to the believer," Messenger began. "The exercise room represents the trials and tests the believer will face. The resting cot represents the peace of God that follows the trials."

31

"I will now speak directly about your world," Influencer emphasized.

"The trials in the life of the believer are as necessary to spiritual growth as exercise is to physical growth. During the trials, the believer must apply the truth of God's Word to the situation he faces. When he relies on a promise found in God's Word that deals with his trial and he experiences God's rescue or wisdom for guidance, he grows in faith similar to how a muscle in an athlete grows in strength. You see, the intake of God's Word simply for information is not the reason He gave it. The believer must follow the heart and soul of God's Word and let it impact the way he lives or it cannot do its work. As an example of those who studied God's truth but didn't let it personally change them, think of the enemies of Christ who had Him crucified. Were they not students of the law of God? Had they not dedicated their lives to the study of God's Word? Even so, it had no impact on them, for they did not apply it to their lives and let it open their eyes to the truth. They failed to let God's Word be their guide for changing their hearts. They were more concerned about show and control. Rather than letting the simple but profound truth in God's Word guide them, they complicated it by substituting their own laws and traditions. They thought they knew God because of their hard, religious, legalistic life, but they couldn't see Him even when He sat and ate with them. These religious zealots missed the coming of their Messiah and the blessing of the true enlightenment found in God's Word, because they didn't apply it to their own lives.

"About the resting cot and its representation," Messenger continued, "the peace of God is symptomatic of being in a right relationship with Him. As an athlete, do you remember how good it felt to be really stretched in your exercise and after the endurance test to finally be able to rest? Do you remember the satisfaction you felt? Do you remember that cool drink of water on a hot day and how wonderful it tasted and felt after a hard workout? Although His peace surpasses comprehension, similar is the peace of God after a trial or test. His peace is a steppingstone in your spiritual maturity, and it is rarely experienced without a trial first."

"Messenger," I asked, "is it really necessary to go through these trials in order to grow?"

"Would you have run laps had your coach not required it? Would you have improved as an athlete had you not run the laps?" Messenger asked. "It is the way with mankind and the believer alike. The believer would settle into a comfortable, stagnant existence and not grow if it were not for tests and trials. God has the power and authority to prevent all trials for His children if He sees fit. But you must understand that God loves you more than you can imagine and His ultimate plan for you is for your own good. God knows all the tiniest details of your life. He

32

knows and understands the pain you go through in your trials, for God the Son faced all those same trials when He lived in your world. But your loving Father will not exempt you from those trials, for He is growing you to Christ-likeness with those spiritual cycles, in which you apply His Word to your trial and experience His rescue or wisdom followed by His resting peace. These cycles are His training regimen by His design and for your spiritual growth. That is why trials and tests are necessary."

Messenger continued, "Many believers stay in their misery rather than trying to find answers from God's Word and letting it change their lives. They stagnate in their spiritual growth because they hold onto their own way of doing things or their own strategy for living. They try to deal with a trial like it was an enemy and attempt to eradicate it by any means, even if it means sin is required. They fail to look inward and upward and ask what God might want to teach them through the trial. Jesus said the fruitful believer would be pruned to bear even more fruit. Pruning hurts but it leads to more blessings and to the ultimate good of the believer. God's Word also says the child of God will be disciplined for his own good in order for him to give up a particular sinful condition he is holding onto. In both cases, pruning or discipline is necessary, for they lead to the fruit of transformation or the fruit of repentance. Both fruits are good. But how sad it is when the believer stops his growth and lives in the misery that stagnation brings to his life."

After Messenger's last comment I could not help but reflect on my own life and how I had struggled with issues of wanting to remain in control rather than entrusting my problem to God. How foolish I had been to think that any solution I could come up with would be better than the one my loving Savior would provide. I didn't realize that the trial I was enduring could have been a blessing of deliverance, either from the known problem or a deeper problem that I was unaware of. Messenger had given me a new slant on looking at my trials and problems. He also interrupted my thoughts when he said:

"Continue to watch the progress in Learner's life and you'll find the area where you have been resisting God. You will also see a common problem that is happening in God's family."

I had forgotten that before I entered this vision, I had asked the Savior how I was resisting Him. I had been so caught up in what I was seeing that I had forgotten the purpose of this vision: to show me who God wanted me to be and how to become that man. Messenger had told me to watch and learn. Therefore, I followed his direction and began to watch intently as Mentor worked with Learner.

Chapter 9

Becoming A Self-Feeder

IT WAS A BEAUTIFUL SIGHT. At first Learner didn't know what to do with the food. He made a mess. But Mentor was patient. Before long Learner got the hang of it and Mentor couldn't get food to his mouth quickly enough. However, like with other newborn babies, the baby food soon wasn't strong enough, especially because of Learner's increased appetite from the exercise. Mentor was always one step ahead of Learner as he moved him down the table. Before long they were at the other end of the table. During this process Learner began to gain weight and put on muscle. Everything about him began to look healthy, from his hair and skin to the shine in his eyes. He was becoming a man right before my eyes. I now understood the value of the nutritional food he was eating, the value of having a gifted teacher like Mentor feed him and the exercise and rest that accompanied the food.

It began to dawn on me that all the feeding to this point was from Mentor to Learner. Learner had not yet been able to feed himself. As this thought ran through my head, Mentor asked Learner a question; Learner nodded. Then Mentor gave Learner a knife and fork and showed him how to use them. It was cumbersome at first, as Learner tried to use these new feeding tools. He also had a hard time deciding where to start with all the food before him. Before long, however, with Mentor's help, Learner began to develop a plan and method for picking out the food he was hungry for. Eventually Learner could discern his own nutritional needs, and all the while Mentor applauded his progress.

As Learner became more skilled in feeding himself, Mentor began to back away and let Learner become more independent. But there were still occasions when Mentor would step forward and suggest that Learner try a food he hadn't tried. I could see that, although Learner was growing into a self-feeder, he still needed the occasional touch of Mentor to help him see things that only years of experience could teach him.

As I watched, a touching scene played out. I even shed a tear. As Learner fed himself, he discovered a special delicacy hidden and overlooked by Mentor. When Learner found it, he couldn't wait to share it with Mentor. I could tell that this touched Mentor, for he perceived that Learner had just entered a new stage in his maturity. I could see that Mentor also received a blessing as the one who once needed to be fed was now feeding the feeder. What a joyful sight!

I was blown away by the progress that Learner had made from the time he had entered the banquet hall. It was especially interesting that when he entered the self-feeding phase, his maturity and muscle mass increased exponentially. He was maturing more rapidly than ever. There was a truth that the Lord wanted to teach me, and it would be found in what I had witnessed. Messenger had said there was a common problem in God's family and that when I was able to see it, I would be able to see where I had been resisting God. I was ready for answers. Before I could ask Messenger to show me the meaning of what I had seen, he spoke.

"Tell me what you have learned so far in this vision," he said.

"Messenger, I realize that this vision is metaphorical for what is happening in my world and the spiritual warfare that is being waged for the soul of mankind. I also realize that God reaches to mankind using believers empowered by the Holy Spirit and the gospel message of God's provision for mankind. I realize that God's provision for mankind is found only through Jesus Christ and the sacrifice He made for us, even though the enemy of our souls would try to convince us otherwise. I realize that once someone comes to God through Jesus Christ, he becomes God's child and it is His purpose and plan to grow the believer to maturity. I realize that God has given His children spiritual gifts to help build His family into maturity. I realize the food that feeds our souls and matures us is God's Word and prayer. Simply put, His Word teaches us how to live."

Before I could continue, Messenger interrupted.

"Now tell me what the banquet table represents."

I answered, "I see that a new believer needs to first be taught from God's Word very gently with the basics by someone who can communicate these truths effectively. I also see that the objective of this teacher should be to increase the new believer's diet of the Word so that he can mature as a result of the deeper and hidden truths that are in God's Word."

Messenger stopped me to emphasize the point with his next question.

"And what about the self-feeding?" Messenger asked.

"I see that this is the ultimate objective for the believer," I answered.

"Well, it's not the ultimate objective, but you can't get there without going through this level of growth," he said.

"You're talking about the Feast in the Inner Chamber again, aren't you?" I asked.

"You're learning," he replied with a smile.

Messenger had posed a question to me about self-feeding, but I wasn't quite sure how to answer it. I knew it was important.

"I need help on that last question," I said.

"Tell me where you are in your own progression on God's banquet table," Messenger asked.

I thought about Learner and tried to compare myself with him in the maturing process. I knew I had crossed the Bridge of Jesus Christ and was a child of God. I knew I was involved with a great church that believed and taught God's Word unashamedly. Therefore, I was comfortable in believing I had gotten beyond the tables of sweets in the courtyard of the Kingdom. I also felt confident that my church and my mentor had done a good job of getting me beyond the baby food stage. Because I was in a great church with a solid Bible teacher, I felt that I had progressed to the point of being able to find real hearty food in the Word and that I was being well fed. I even thought I was exercising a little faith every now and then, and had been growing spiritually. But it was at the next point in comparing my progression to Learner's that I began to grow uncomfortable, for I saw where my maturing process had ended. I became painfully aware that I still needed to be fed God's Word by someone else and that I was not a self-feeder. The sober truth was that I had stopped maturing spiritually.

I wasn't surprised by Messenger's next question:

"Do you now see the problem? This problem is not only with you but also with most of God's family. You have not yet become a self-feeder, so you cannot go to the Feast in the Inner Chamber. It is at this point in your spiritual journey that you are resisting God and He cannot mature you into the man He wants you to be."

I asked, "Why do we do this to ourselves? Why do I do it to myself?"

"There are several reasons, but it's mostly spiritual laziness," Messenger answered. "There is another common problem. Some teachers, by design or neglect, do not teach God's children to become self-feeders, and they keep His children dependent on spoon-feeding. These teachers don't seem to understand that, even though they might be serious and diligent in their efforts to teach about God, unless their work eventually points and encourages God's child to become a self-feeder, their ministry is woefully incomplete and disrupts the process God has designed. By keeping God's child dependent on spoon-feeding, spiritual stagnation results, and the teacher is not raising up co-laborers who could join him in his ministry. Both the teacher and the believer are hurt. It is absolutely necessary for God's child to become a self-feeder if he is to become spiritually mature."

"Why is it necessary?" I asked simply.

"Consider how God's Word answers that question," Messenger replied.

He quoted, "How can a young man keep his way pure? By keeping it according to Thy Word. Thy Word I have treasured in my heart, that I may not sin against Thee."

Next he quoted, "Stand firm, therefore, HAVING GIRDED YOUR LOINS WITH TRUTH, and HAVING PUT ON THE BREASTPLATE OF RIGHTEOUSNESS and having SHOD YOUR FEET WITH THE PREPARATION OF THE GOSPEL OF PEACE; in addition to all, taking up the shield of faith with which you will be able to extinguish all the flaming missiles of the evil one. And take THE HELMET OF SALVATION, and the sword of the Spirit, which is the Word of God."

"I could give you many more answers from God's Word that would answer your question, but your vision will not last long enough. The simple answer you need is that God's Word is full of treasure that is ready to be mined by the seeker. In His Word the believer will find everything he needs for living, for truly prospering, for dealing with disappointments, failures, successes and any circumstance that a child of God will face. God's Word is His instrument for drawing the believer to the intimacy available with Him for His children. God's Word contains His love letters to His children. These love letters and His instructions are often hidden from plain view, and it requires a sincere, dedicated effort to find these truths. His Word is alive with truth for any moment in time for any believer in need. God's Word reveals His provision for mankind by pointing to His Son. His Word also gives His children instructions for joining Him in the harvest for the souls of mankind. God's Word is His shield of protection for His children and is the 'Sword of the Spirit,' in that it empowers the believer with the major offensive weapon for the spiritual warfare he faces. God's Word instills in the believer the courage for the fight and the weapons for winning the battles."

I personalized my next question. "Why do I need to become a self-feeder, Messenger?"

Messenger looked me in the eye as he emphasized the next point. "For you, child of God, are in danger, and there is much to lose if you do not get stronger. You are weak and vulnerable, and so are those around you because of it. The Lord wants to use you for greater purposes that will bless your world and you beyond your understanding, but He cannot do so until your defenses are stronger. He wants you to be His hands, His voice and His love to those around you, but you cannot, for you know not. Until your spiritual diet is increased, you cannot become the man God wants you to be, for you do not know how to battle the enemy of mankind. You cannot serve God as you should or could, because you have stopped growing in your likeness to Christ. Your spiritual growth is retarded, because you have not become a self-feeder."

As Messenger's words lingered in my ears, I thought of how many times I had cheated myself of God's blessings by not following His plans for me. But I never realized the danger I flirted with. I had grown to regret the many times I tried to short-circuit His plans by launching out on my own and not following His advice. I could see that my spiritual laziness was the cause of my immaturity. I had found it so easy to get all of my feeding in God's Word from the great teaching I received in church. But this diet was not enough to grow me. In fact, it was barely enough to sustain me, evidenced by the way I would fall back toward my old sinful nature as the week passed. I could now see that my spiritual diet was so insufficient that I was anemic. I could see that it wouldn't take much to trip me up. This scared me as I remembered the invisible, hideous creatures that waged war against mankind and against me. I grasped the truth that my armor would not stand against a strong attack from this enemy, and I had to do something about it. I was beginning to sweat as I saw the gravity of my situation. It wasn't just a case of spiritual immaturity, although that is important. It was a case of soul-threatening vulnerability. I recognized that I couldn't be the spiritual leader for my family, friends and the people in my life if I wasn't maturing. I knew that my prayers were as weak or as strong as my spiritual maturity and, at present, they were as anemic as I was. With great earnestness I cried:

"Messenger, I'm ready to move to the next level. I realize that I must take the initiative to become a self-feeder. I don't want to be, or the people around me to be, in danger anymore because of my spiritual laziness. I'm scared with how vulnerable we are because of my immaturity. I'm ready to return home and start this process in earnest. I want to be the man God wants me to be. I want to be a spiritual warrior for my family and the people around me. Please, I've got to get back and start growing. Take me home. I've got to get back."

Messenger's calming words settled me for the moment. "Your vision is not yet complete. For you to be the man you speak of, more than self-feeding is required. It is essential in the process, but more is required. Follow Learner and you will see the man whom God will make of you and how this will happen when you partake of the Feast in the Inner Chamber."

"Finally," I thought, "I am going to see the Feast in the Inner Chamber."

Chapter 10

The Feast

I WATCHED LEARNER RISE from the banquet table, where he had been eating. I followed him as he walked toward two large wooden doors that exited from the banquet hall. Over the large doors were inscribed these words:

> He Who Enters This Chamber Must Do So By
> Personal Abandonment and Absolute Trust

I watched Learner pause and read the words. I could tell he was considering the impact that such a commitment would have on his life. This was a serious, life-changing challenge, and it could not be entered into without considering the cost. I couldn't help but think he was remembering where he had come from, outside the Kingdom's walls, and his process of development since then. I thought, "He has to realize that the One Who has loved him and brought him this far would never ask anything of him that would hurt him or betray him even with the challenge that is being asked of him." After a while of contemplation, Learner nodded as if to assure himself of the things I had come to think. Then he opened the massive doors and walked into the Chamber.

I was behind Learner as the doors opened, and I could see the contents of the Inner Chamber. The room was not big. It could even be described as cozy. The walls were richly paneled with beautiful woodwork. On the walls hung pieces of shining armor, swords and fighting equipment. On the far wall was a large stone fireplace with a blazing fire. Over the mantle was a large shield with the emblem of a lion and a lamb. The wood floor and the paneled walls reflected a soft, golden glow from the fire, which was the room's source of light. In front of the fireplace, two comfortable-looking overstuffed chairs faced each other. If not for the room's warmth, this could have been some kind of war room because of the armament on the walls. This was no war room in a traditional sense, but one could sense that many battles had been prepared for in this room by the strategies that would have been discussed in those two chairs.

I was eagerly moving to the entrance to follow Learner when Messenger blocked my way.

"You cannot enter this time and place with Learner," he said. "It is reserved only for Learner."

As he spoke, the massive doors began to close.

"I will explain to you what is happening so you will know what to expect if you choose to enter the Feast in the Inner Chamber," Messenger stated.

"Why could I not join Learner in the Chamber?" I asked.

Messenger replied, "The Feast in the Inner Chamber is a private and deeply spiritual time for Learner. It is not to be observed, but experienced. You will understand this firsthand should you choose to go forward in your spiritual journey upon returning to your world. Now, for your understanding."

Messenger continued, "Note the inscription on the doors. Before you enter this special time and place, personal abandonment and absolute trust are required. Personal abandonment is another description of the 'living sacrifice' mentioned in God's Word. Another way to describe it is to say it includes all that one is or ever hopes to be, all that one has or ever hopes to have; all personal rights to oneself, all personal aspirations and all aspects of one's life are left behind. For this reason, Learner paused to contemplate the cost of the decision he was about to make."

The commitment level required for going into the Feast in the Inner Chamber frightened me. Messenger must have sensed this, for his eyes began to show compassion again. Then he said:

"Child of God, I sense that you are disturbed about this requirement. Let me explain to you better what it means so that you can look beyond the initial fear and see the joyful future. Do you remember your question to the Father before you entered this vision? You asked what you must do to enter the Feast in the Inner Chamber. The Father replied that you must let go of trying to keep control of your life. It is that futile attempt at control that keeps you from taking the next step. Control of one's life is only an illusion anyway. Only Sovereign God can be in complete control. The question is, do you want God to be the Master of your life and control it, or do you want to continue your futile attempts to do so? To 'abandon' means to leave behind the attempt to be your own master."

He continued, "Have you not yet grasped the message in Learner's journey? Anything he has forfeited has been made up many times over by the good and perfect plans of the Savior of his soul. God's objective is to bless the believer who abandons his life into the safekeeping of the loving Father, not to punish him for doing so. It is the enemy of the believer who would try to convince him otherwise."

I was feeling a little better because of Messenger's words. I thought of Learner's decision time and how I also had felt he needed to remember God's record with him. I thought Learner needed to rely on the same God who had taken him safely thus far and would be with him beyond those doors. I have come to understand that we all can be bold with our theories when it's someone else who faces the test. But, when it came home to me and I had to apply it to myself, it revealed my cowardice. Because of Messenger, I could see the great benefit of encouragement from one who had been through those doors, and lived to tell about it. I could see how his authenticity and experience could instill courage to the timid as he shared his own life story about God's blessings after he went through those doors.

"Messenger, why did I become so frightened initially when you explained the commitment of abandonment?" I asked.

"Have you forgotten your current spiritual condition? Do you understand better now how God's Word instills courage and why you need to become a self-feeder?" he answered. "What has been revealed to you is that you are not ready to enter the Feast in the Inner Chamber. When you grow spiritually as a result of feeding on God's Word, your experience with trials, and then His peace that comes after deliverance, there will come a point when your expectations of God's faithfulness will override this fear. Then you will be ready to enter through the doors, and into the Feast in the Inner Chamber. Now, let me continue to help you understand."

Messenger paused, then continued: "To 'trust absolutely' is the other requirement for entering the Feast in the Inner Chamber. If abandonment is the act of emptying one's hand of the illusion of control, trust is the act of grasping what Almighty God has to give back. Trusting absolutely is to trust in total, without reservation. It is the act of grasping, with both hands, He Who Is Able. It is the act of grasping God's best without trying to keep one hand on another remedy. It is likened to flying from a trapeze without a safety net with the complete confidence that your Catcher will never fail you as you leave the bar and depend on Him. This is another level of trust. The challenges to have this kind of trust will be monumental, but so will be the rewards. The greatest reward will be to enjoy the Feast in the Inner Chamber."

By this time I had heard enough about the Feast in the Inner Chamber. I wanted to know what to expect. I had seen the great feast that was set up on the banquet table, and I couldn't wait to see what the other feast would look like. I was a little confused by what I had seen when I peeked into the Chamber. Instead of seeing another banquet table of food waiting for Learner, I saw only two chairs. I thought, "Maybe this will be a catered affair, where servers will bring in the food after the doors are closed."

I couldn't wait any longer, so I asked Messenger, "About the Feast in the Inner Chamber: Where's the food? I looked through the Chamber door and saw only two chairs. What's going on in there with Learner?"

"Oh, there's food, all right, but the food he is partaking of has more spiritual nutritional value than anything Learner has ever partaken of. He is being prepared to be the great warrior that God wants him to be. He is being strengthened with wisdom from God and the courage to face any foe. With this Feast he is being fitted with his suit of armor and the insight with how to use his spiritual weapons when he emerges from the Feast. In this Chamber, Learner has no distractions and is maturing even faster than all previous stages in his development."

Messenger paused before beginning his next statement:

"You were expecting a continuation of the spiritual food that Learner was partaking of in the banquet hall. Therefore, you were surprised to see that there wasn't a banquet table waiting for him. Understand that everything Learner was partaking of in the banquet hall was leading him to the Feast in the Inner Chamber. All of the spiritual food he was taking in before going into the Chamber was making him hungrier for the Feast ahead.

All the spiritual food was placing in him a desire for something beyond what he was experiencing. In the Chamber, Learner is finding what he has craved all his life. In the Chamber, Learner is partaking of the Feast that all mankind is starving for. The Feast that Learner is partaking of right now is the Lord God, Himself."

Messenger's words hit me like a ton of bricks. I was surprised that this was the meaning of the Feast in the Inner Chamber, but it made perfect sense. I could see how all of God's efforts have been to bring mankind back to Himself. I could see that He is not satisfied, nor should we be, with a beginning salvation experience. It is His purpose to draw us deeper and deeper into our relationship with Him. I could see that it is out of that deepening, intimate relationship that the supernatural is transferred to the ordinary. This was the message Jesus was giving us when He said we must abide in Him and He in us. The transformation in the believer's life comes by this abiding with Him, and it is in this abiding fellowship that He imparts His characteristics and values. The Feast in the Inner Chamber is, in truth, the time we spend in this abiding fellowship with Christ. Yes, it all began to make sense.

At this point I was exhausted with the truth I had been exposed to. I wanted to go home. I was ready to get to the self-feeding phase of my life and prepare to enter the Feast in the Inner Chamber. As I was about to ask Messenger again to take me back, he spoke.

"Watch what happens next."

The doors to the Inner Chamber began to open slowly. I was to the side of the doors, so I could only see the emergence of the man who came from the Chamber. I couldn't believe my eyes. Standing before me was a man in shining armor similar to Influencer. I recognized him as Learner, but he had only a slight similarity to the man who entered God's Kingdom. The man who had entered God's kingdom was replaced by a new one. It was obvious that an amazing supernatural transformation had occurred in Learner's life and that the Feast he had just partaken of had completed its work. This new man now stood strong, confident and dangerous. He was ready for battle.

Learner began to walk toward the doors leading from the banquet hall. He walked with a newfound confidence and determination. Messenger motioned for me to follow.

Learner walked through the doors, and out of the castle. At the foot of the stairs, Influencer was waiting with two beautiful horses, which also were dressed for battle. One of the horses was Influencer's; the other was for Learner. I began to realize that the process of expressing the gospel was about to be repeated, just like what Influencer had done with Learner when he was a refugee. Learner and Influencer were about to go on a mission from the Kingdom of God in search of another refugee whom God was calling to the Kingdom.

Influencer and Learner were excited about their mission, for they were ready and fit for battle. These men were prepared; they knew clearly what their mission would entail and how to fight the battles they would face. These men had to be frightening warriors to their enemies. I was glad they were on my side.

Just after Learner mounted his steed but before he left the courtyard, Messenger moved directly in front of me and looked me straight in the eye. He asked, "Do you understand all that you have seen in this vision?"

I nodded, although there was still much to contemplate.

Then with a serious tone Messenger asked, "Are you ready to see the man the Father wants to make of you?"

I had gotten so caught up in Learner's development that I had forgotten this was the original objective of the vision. I wanted to see the man God wanted to make of me. I answered, "Yes, I do."

Messenger continued, "Do you remember that I told you at the start of your vision that Refugee was the inner man of someone you are familiar with?"

I did remember, but I had let it pass because I couldn't see a resemblance to anyone I knew.

"Child of God," he said, "the Father has given you a great blessing. He is allowing you to see the man you can be if you will make your way to the Feast in the Inner Chamber. Once you have emerged from the Feast, you will be given the great blessing of helping other men find their way to this Feast. Now, behold the man you can become."

As Messenger's words trailed off, Learner's face began to transform. There, mounted on his beast of war, dressed in shining armor and ready for battle, was the man I had been following through his spiritual journey to the Feast in the Inner Chamber. Little did I know when I first saw the pitiful Refugee, who later became Learner that I was looking at someone most familiar to me. Before my eyes, mounted on his horse and courageously ready for battle, was the man God wanted me to become. It was also the man I desired to be. I was looking at a man that was slightly older than me. But, I was looking at myself.

If there was ever a moment in my life when disappointment and excitement could coexist, it was then. Yes, the revelation of my spiritual retardation and the resulting loss of joy and purpose disappointed me. But at the same time I was excited about the hope of tomorrow and the clear purpose before me. The thought that I could be a warrior like Learner and Influencer excited me. With great resolve I committed to change things. I turned to tell Messenger about my commitment only to see that I was rising to the clouds and being withdrawn from him and the vision. As I slowly rose, I could see that Learner and Influencer had already entered the battleground. Arrows were bouncing off their armor as quickly as they were being shot. I could see the joy in their faces as their swords were drawn and being used to attack the enemy of mankind. Like the expression of sheer delight seen in the faces of athletes when they run for the prize, these two warriors had the expression of joy and satisfaction. It was the last scene in the vision as I was drawn back to the clouds and then to my study.

Chapter 11

The Journey Begins

I OPENED MY EYES. I was still lying on the floor of the study, wrapped in my blanket. The storm was still active. I thought the vision would have lasted days. However, looking at the clock, I could see I had been away only a few minutes. My heart was pumping as I thought through the vision.

As I began to calm down, I became tranquil. The wind blowing in the trees and through the window screens threatened to chill me. But I was warm and comfortable as I lay wrapped in the blanket. Before long I drifted into a restful sleep that had evaded me for weeks.

The next morning I awakened to the smell of brewing coffee. Our three children were wild with excitement. The storm had dumped eight inches of powdery snow, closing schools and roads. As with the children, I was excited about this forced "day off" for I had much to do for following up the vision I had received only a few hours before.

After sharing with my wife what had happened, I called my pastor and the man who had introduced me to Christ. I was relieved after I had shared my vision with them that it was not met with skepticism. Instead, I received a hardy encouragement to follow through with my new commitment.

Next I started praying that God would bring to my mind some men who would go with me on my journey to maturity.

I realized that I needed other men to encourage me and keep me accountable in my goal to become a self-feeder. I've come to understand that an important requirement for personal growth is to serve someone else. I couldn't think of a better thing to do for another person than to help him get to the Feast in the Inner Chamber. So it was with an attitude of both serving and being helped that I excitedly called the men who came to mind.

Most of the men I talked to that day were home because of the snow. Therefore, it was with a relaxed and easy manner that I shared my desire to go on a spiritual

49

journey and discover what it means to go deeper in intimacy with Christ. I asked them to go with me, so that we could help each other. It struck a note of harmony in all of the men I talked to, and each said he had been struggling with the same concerns and desire to move forward; they just hadn't known what to do next. The things I shared from my vision answered their questions about how to start, so they were all for it.

We started meeting together weekly with the purpose of prayer, the study of God's Word and accountability. After a while we began to see changes in each of us, as God's precepts began to guide us. Old angers and memories of wrongs began to pass away. Personal wounds were exposed, prayed for and eradicated. Our family relationships began to grow stronger, and our joy began to increase. At this point we understood that God had given us an invitation to come closer to Him and to understand what it means to be under His leadership and the benefits of His care.

Though this group journey, we all grew closer to the Feast in the Inner Chamber. Our initial strategy for helping one another become self-feeders was for each participant to simply find something new and fresh from the Word and bring it to the weekly meeting. This accountability forced us to dig into Scripture and be prepared. The great thing about this is the more we have done it, the more we have become captivated by the wisdom and insight found in Scripture. Most of us have concluded that it's something we can no longer live without, even if there were no accountability. It has become normal to rise early and prepare for the day by feasting on God's Word. We are starting to learn what it means to be a "self-feeder."

As we have all moved closer to the doors to the Inner Chamber we have faced the natural fear that precedes the level of commitment required to enter them. Each of us individually must face and deal with our own obstacles. However, we have found that Christ wants us to deal with these fears and obstacles in our own way, and when we are ready. Our first steps to the Inner Chamber require that we become self-feeders and this prepares us for the next step.

Looking back now, I realize that at this point in my journey most of what I was learning was still theoretical to me, personally. It had to start there, but it couldn't remain there. In order to make these promises from God real to me personally, just as was explained in the "exercise room" in the Kingdom, I would be given a series of tests to drive home the theories and turn them into experience. I have come to understand that God builds experience with tests and He is not content with our mere knowledge of facts. He is more concerned with our relationship with Him rather than our knowledge of Him and it is through the testing process we journey closer to Him.

After several months of pursuing a deeper understanding of God in His Word, the next step in my spiritual journey was to be taken through the testing process I speak of, and it was there that I would discover the truth of those things He had been teaching me in His Word. I would discover that the journey is not for the fainthearted. But, I would also discover that the Prize of the Universe was waiting for me at every point in my journey.

Just like Messenger had promised, at the end of the testing process the King was waiting for me in the Inner Chamber. But it was up to me to make the final step through the doors of "Personal Abandonment and Absolute Trust." At this point I didn't know what that meant, and if I were ready. But, my journey had begun, and there was no turning back for me. My journey had to continue all the way through the doors, and I was about to face the decision required to make that next step. However, before I would be asked to make that step I would be shown another example of the man God wanted me to become. Like the vision that represented to me the hidden world that we do not see, God showed me an example of a man who would be overlooked and obscure in our world, as well. But what is not seen in a man such as this, is the hidden power that is within him and the incredible power of God that is at his disposal because he resides in the Inner Chamber. I would be led to one of these champions and I would see what a true Influencer looks like. It would be a surprise to me, for he would not fall into the stereotypical image of one who we would think as "influential." But, his life would be used to give me the courage to make the next step and I would understand the hidden work that God can do with a man that lives with Him in the Inner Chamber.

PART TWO

Chapter 12

The Getaway

IT HAD BEEN SEVERAL MONTHS since the vision. There was no doubt in my mind that God had revealed to me a path that would take me into a deeper intimacy with Him. I had already begun to see changes in my life, as I studied God's Word and let His precepts guide me. My efforts were cumbersome at first. However, with the encouragement of the group of men who shared their own spiritual journey with mine, we were able to encourage each other and gain ground. As good as this period was, I knew deep down that I had to face some challenges ahead that would either make or break me, or do both. I also knew that I would be facing my challenges without those men and my decisions would be wrestled within the privacy of my inner world. It was with this mind-set that I took time off from my busy schedule to sort things out and seek an understanding of what my next step would be.

It had been my desire for a while to make a weekend hike on an old, deserted, logging trail that I had heard about the year before. I was told that the trail led into a mountain range four hours drive from my house, and was rarely used except by hunters when the deer or turkey season was open. Since it was winter and between seasons, I expected to see no one, which is what I hoped for. Therefore, with the troubling motivation fresh on my mind, I loaded my four-wheel drive truck, kissed my wife and children good by and headed to the mountains.

My wife had already begun to see many changes. She could see a contrasting difference in me after the vision and understood that I would not want to get away for a weekend alone, unless it was really needed. If there was a person who was my Number One encourager and cheerleader, it was my wife. She had a spiritual instinct about her that was very discerning and supportive. She is a prayer warrior and spends many early morning hours praying for her family and others on her prayer list. I could tell that she was not surprised when I discussed my desire to get away. She simply gave me the encouragement that I needed to go.

Now, when I chisel out a time on my calendar for something like this get-a-way, I don't let many things get in the way. My busy time schedule creates a lot of urgency in me to follow through and make things happen. However, following through with things is also part of my make-up, since I'm rather goal-oriented. It's an asset to me most of the time. On this trip, it almost got me killed.

I had looked with disinterest at the weather reports, for I couldn't imagine anything that would be big enough to keep me from changing my plans. There were some vague reports about a winter storm that would be passing to the west of our home town. It never lodged in my mind that the area the reports were speaking of was the very area where I would be spending the weekend. It was a beautiful, unusually mild, winter day when I left our house. I was lulled into thinking I would be facing similar weather the next few days. Man, was I wrong!

I took my customary camping gear along, including a down sleeping bag, a change of socks, several cans of beans, water, an aluminum fry pan, flashlight, a one-man tent and a small, 3-weight fly rod. I like to travel light, for I planned a long hike on the mountain trail. But, when it comes to a good meal, the extra weight for the food and cooking is worth it.

After three hours of driving, I began to view the mountains. The sight of their majestic stance on the horizon caused my pulse to quicken with excitement. Sometime later, I found the deserted logging road that I was looking for.

Before heading up the logging trail, I shifted the truck into fourwheel drive and began a rough ascent. After an hour of driving up this trail, I came to an impassable place in the road and decided to park the truck and begin my hike at this point. So far, since leaving the paved highway over two hours before, I had seen no other human beings. I was totally alone.

In looking back on that adventure, I realize that I could have been in a terrible position if something unexpected, such as an accident, had happened to me on this hike. However, at this point in the journey, my mind was about as far away as it could have been from any problems. I could only smell the freshness of the pine and fir trees. Birds were active, as they enjoyed the uncharacteristic warmth of the day. Squirrels eased out of their winter nests and joined other forest creatures that ventured out. Even though I was alone, I felt God's creation was all around me and I was given permission to simply enjoy it and Him.

In my journey into intimacy with my Savior, I have discovered that learning to enjoy Him is not only one of the great benefits of redemption, it is also essential to my spiritual growth. Like many hard-driving individuals, I have had a hard time understanding and practicing the necessity of this privilege. It generally requires the pressures of a busy lifestyle or circumstantial challenges to drive me to getting a time alone with my Savior so that I can cry out for help. What a shame it is that His children require desperation before we will give in to our basic need for having special times of intimacy with the Lord. But, I am learning and even more after this trip.

As I continued on my hike, I came to a stream that I was hoping I would find. Although the beans for supper are acceptable after being heated on a campfire, nothing is better than fresh caught and cooked mountain trout to go with them. I could see trout lurking at the base of the rapids in the clear water. So I unpacked my rod and reel and tied my favorite sinking fly on the tippet. After casting upstream, I let the fly bump the bottom of the rapids, all along stripping the line through my fingers to take the slack out of the line. After a few moments, a hungry trout latched onto the fly and my lightweight rod bent. Because I was using a very light tippet, I had to play the trout until he was ready to give in. Finally, he rolled over on his side and allowed me to ease him close to the shore. "What a beauty!" I exclaimed as I lifted him from the water.

I normally catch and release my fish unless I am seeking food, which was the case this evening. After a few more casts, I had secured another trout and was ready to find a good place to start a fire and set up camp. The wind was starting to shift and I could sense by its change that a new weather pattern was in store. Because of this, I looked for a place to block the north wind and to prop up my small tent. I didn't have to go far before I found an ideal place.

I quickly created a campfire pit and placed rocks around it. Dry twigs and fallen limbs were abundant. So, I had no problem getting the fire started and fed. I placed my aluminum fry pan on some rocks close to the fire and melted a small, pat of butter in the pan. I placed the opened canned beans next to the fire, cleaned the fish and placed them in the pan. Before long, the smell of supper was making me realize that I hadn't eaten all day and I was hungry.

As my meal was cooking on the campfire, I then turned my attention to unfolding my tent and getting it ready for a night's sleep. About the time I finished smoothing the ground and setting the tent up, it was time to turn the trout in the pan. Like I said, I'm efficient when I have a goal. There is no better motivation than a stomach that wants to be fed.

After a few more minutes of cooking, the beans and fish were ready to be enjoyed. I moved the fish to one side of the pan and poured the can of beans in with them. I ate from the pan until my hunger was satisfied, which was after the pan had been completely cleaned of its contents.

After I finished my feast and cleaned the pan in the nearby stream, I unfolded my sleeping bag and brought it close to the campfire. I propped my back on a nearby boulder and allowed myself to enjoy the remaining traces of daylight, as the sun moved below the western horizon.

"Lord," I prayed, "I am grateful for the great meal that I was just given. I can't think of anything that would have satisfied me more than the fish and beans. I thank You for this great camping spot, a safe drive up to the mountains, and a precious family that encouraged me to get to these woods and hopefully find some answers."

I paused my prayer and looked at the stars while noticing the clouds were moving more quickly now. Then I continued my prayer.

"Father, there is something that has been troubling me. I have learned to heed Your call to get away and to listen to You. Therefore, my request of You is that I will hear You, as You speak to my innermost being. Help me to tune in. Make me sensitive to Your voice. Lord, if there is anything in me that is a hindrance and is hurting my fellowship with You, show me what it is so that I can let go of it. If there is a different path that I must take, show me that path and I will follow You."

As I voiced this prayer I leaned against the boulder and listened to the crackling fire. The fresh fallen limbs still had a little sap in them and this livened the fire with some pops and spews. Yes, I was weary from the long day. But, I was relaxed, no longer hungry, and I was receiving much-needed restoration from my King.

I am learning that prayer should not be a formal thing that is rigid and contrived. In fact, I think that these type prayers are an insult to God sometimes, especially when it is rote and without a heartfelt beseeching of God. Oh, we need to take our prayers very serious and with reverence as we approach the King of Kings. But we need to enjoy our conversation with our Savior and desire that He enjoy us. For a long time I struggled with the concept of praying constantly, as is encouraged in the Bible. He is showing me that this is just, in fact, conversing with Him as I go through my day and deal with the things before me. He wants to be involved with me in the details of my life, and with every aspect of it. This takes a lot of the formality out of my prayer time. But, it gives me a perspective that my best friend is with me, and I am welcome to voice my prayer as a friend does to another friend. I realize my Friend is the Lord God Himself and I should always keep this in mind. Being familiar with God? Yes. Being disrespectful and attempting to pull Him down to my level? Absolutely not!

I shared this thought with a man who had not yet discovered this truth, as he was still holding on to his prayer rote as if his religion depended on it. He asked me if I was "too casual with God and if I forget Who He is by not addressing Him properly." My response was that it is just the opposite. When I draw near to my Savior and really see Who He is, I cannot help being awed by His splendor and majesty. His invitation to His children is through His unconditional love called "grace," and this takes away the need for legalism on our part. Prayer is our communication with Him. It is our adoring response, as we recognize Who He is. I don't know if my explanation satisfied the man. But I know it has broken down many barriers in my own prayer life. I now enjoy my Savior and converse with Him as never before.

As I sat next to the campfire and reflected on God's mercy and grace to me and how He has led me to a deeper intimacy with Him, I could feel His pleasure and His presence. However, my thoughts were being distracted, for the wind was picking up bringing with it a new chill. The clouds had now thickened, covering any light from the moon. My relaxation time was challenged with a sickening feeling that I might be facing something I hadn't bargained for. While dwelling briefly on this thought, I tossed another small log on the fire and stoked up the flame. This countered the chill for a while.

Before long, the contrasting cold front collided with the warm moist southern air that we had been enjoying for several days, and the inevitable outcome was produced. Snow. It started with a few flakes and then erupted into one of the quickest and heaviest downfalls I have ever seen.

I decided it was time to get out of the weather, so I put my sleeping bag and other gear inside the tent.

I tested the rigging to make sure they were all firm, for the wind was really picking up. One last look around and I escaped into the little one-man tent. I spread the ground pad and the down sleeping bag, and quickly slipped into it. I could tell that the night would be a challenge to keep warm, and hopefully the tent wouldn't fall in on me. I was glad that I placed it so that it was protected from a frontal assault by the north wind.

Now, I must be honest. I liked it. I don't know what it is or where it comes from. But, I like to snuggle in a warm sleeping bag when there is a noisy storm going on outside the tent. I suppose it could be the contrast of the cold outside and warmth in the sleeping bag. It could be a survival instinct that comes to the surface or some crazy childhood fantasy being lived out. I just know that I sleep in a cozy state even though I spend most of the night aware of the storm noise around me.

As I folded my arms under my neck while lying on my back, I began to think about that stormy night the year before. It was a similar storm front that rolled in that roused me from bed. However, it wasn't the storm that had wakened me, for I had been struggling with sleep disruption for a while. No, it was the turmoil that was churning inside me that woke me. I will always remember that night for it was then the Lord gave me the vision.

The vision! Man, did that change my life. I can look back now and see that it was after the vision my life began to really change. It was as real as anything I had ever seen or encountered. For over a year, I had been practicing some of the things that I learned in the vision. As a result, I have been helped in my spiritual growth and I can see the difference. Best of all, others see it and appreciate the changes. But, now there seems to be something else that I am being urged to do. It is likened to a child that has been wading into the water up to his waist and now his father is asking him to move into the deep water. He's scared, but he trusts his father. Likewise, I feel God urging me to a deeper trust in Him. It scares me, but I am learning to trust God's heart. I'm not sure what it is that I need to do, or release or to grasp. That's why I'm here. I'm searching for answers. I'm here to listen to God and seek His guidance. However, right now all I can hear is the snowstorm picking up. Thank the Lord I have a warm, dry place to hunker down and ride it out for the night. Hopefully it would play itself out and I could resume my hike. However, it was looking doubtful.

I closed my eyes and prayed, "Father, I'm here to listen to You. I feel Your leadership to trust You more; but, I'm not really sure how to do this. I feel Your delight, as I have grown closer to You. I want to grow even closer and become the man that You want me to be and the one who can serve You best. I realize that I cannot do it on my own. I need Your hand on me to accomplish this. But, I also know that I play a part. I need to know what that part is so that I can do it. Father, lead me this night and these next days to know what steps I need to take next."

After my prayer, I began to think about the vision and try to recall the things Messenger said to me. They seemed so clear at the time. But after a year, I was cloudy on some of the points. I was hoping the Lord would help me understand what I need to do.

It was in that time when the body relaxes and starts to fall to sleep, but right before losing consciousness, that I remembered the writing on the doorposts: "He Who Enters This Chamber Must Do So By Personal Abandonment and Absolute Trust." It was like a flash before my eyes. When this happened, somehow I knew that this was the key I was looking for.

As I reflected on the words on the doorposts to the Inner Chamber, I began to doze off. The long ride, the satisfying meal and the noise of the storm lulled me to sleep. My last words before dropping off were, "Lord, show me what it means to abandon myself to You and to trust You absolutely." With that, I wrapped snugly in my sleeping bag, and went to sleep.

Chapter 13

The Great Escape

THE STORM CONTINUED THROUGH THE NIGHT but it did not concern me, for I was warm and comfortable. I slept soundly. However, just before waking, I heard these words spoken clearly to me, and in fact it was when I heard them that I opened my eyes.

"Wisdom will speak. But, you must listen with your heart, not with your mind. Listen to My servant and he will guide you," is what I heard.

I was startled by the clarity of these words as I thought the voice came from someone who was actually right next to me. When I awoke, I realized that I was in the tent and I had slept through the night without waking.

As I thought about the voice and its message, I became aware of the penetrating cold that was touching my exposed face. Since I had snuggled deeply into my sleeping bag, I had not felt the drastic drop in the temperature. Now that I was awake and exposed to the cold, I realized that this could be a life-threatening situation if I did not act quickly to get back to my truck and head home.

I put my extra shirt and socks on and then realized that other than that, I had no other extra cloths to insulate me from the cold. I had not prepared for this event. I looked out the tent, and estimated that about 10 inches of snow had fallen during the night. There was currently a brief lull in the downfall, but the clouds were heavy and promising more of the same.

I left my tent and other things and brought only my sleeping bag as I wrapped it around my head and shoulders. The hike through the snow was a struggle, as I had to literally wade through the powder. It didn't take long before my feet began to feel the effect and ache from the cold. It was good that I was constantly moving, keeping the circulation going, for this kept them from going numb. It was a three-hour struggle to keep going and stay on a path hidden by the snow; but I finally made it back to the truck just before the storm erupted again. The storm was blowing with a fury as the snow was being driven in a horizontal flight. I cranked the truck and was thankful it started. While the truck warmed up, I cleared the windows of the massive amounts of snow that had collected on them during the night. Then I headed down the mountain.

Following the old lumber trail back down the mountain was a slow endeavor as I picked my way through hidden ruts. There were times I could only guess that I was on the trail. Three hours later I was relieved to see the farm road that led to the highway; however, my relief was short-lived as I could see the effects of the snowstorm on the open road and fields. I had just emerged from the mountains, where the trees had caught and broken up the snowdrifts. In the open fields that stood at the base of the mountains, snowdrifts were piled high over the roads. I could not distinguish between the fields, the road and the ditches. Compounding the problem was the driving snow that limited my visibility.

I offered a silent prayer for my escape from the mountains. I realized that I had been in great danger and many things could have happened on my return down the mountain that could have been disastrous. Coexisting in me at the time was a sense of relief and a sense of foreboding. Relief, in that I had made it safe thus far; foreboding, as I assessed the rest of my trip home.

I turned my truck onto the road and did my best to straddle its middle. It was hit or miss if this was being done, for there was no way I could reference what was road or what was ditch. For two hours it was road. For that last minute it was ditch as my front tire fell off the road and pulled the truck into the deep ditch.

Chapter 14

The Farmhouse

NOW, I'VE TRAVELED A LOT over my career; a regular "road warrior." You would think I would know better, but I let my common sense be pushed aside on this trip. I would normally never start a long drive without checking the weather first and what the driving conditions down the road would be. I would surely never go off on a camping trip if I had known what would happen. But, in my haste to get away, I let all those things slip my mind. It was quite a slip as the largest snowfall recorded in the last 20 years was dumped on the area I was in. Little did I know that 24 hours after leaving my home, I would find myself stranded in a ditch next to a lonely country farm road looking for shelter from the monstrous weather I would face. I look back now and can see Sovereign God's hand redirecting my journey and taking me to the answer to my prayer of the night before, but, it was a frightening experience to get to that point.

I tried to dislodge the truck but a strange noise made me realize that something was wrong underneath the truck. I dug through the snow and could see that the axle had been broken. Compounding the problem was a cracked radiator. The antifreeze was pouring out. A sickening feeling in my stomach came as I assessed my situation. I would not be able to spend the night in the truck and in a few hours I would be frozen by the deathly cold I was feeling.

I looked at my watch and realized that it was only a few minutes before dark. It couldn't get much darker though, for the storm was at its peak. I could barely make out my surroundings. The wind was cutting through me like a knife. I knew that I needed to find shelter and find it immediately. I was beginning to feel desperate. I was frightened. For the first time, it hit me that I could really be facing a life or death situation.

"Jesus," I prayed, "You have delivered me from some terrible circumstances in the past. None have been this dangerous. Even so, I know that You can give me what I need to survive. I can see no way out of this, but, I trust You and accept what You want for me, whether its life or death. Open my eyes to Your way, Father, and I will walk in it. If You choose not to do this, I ask You to close my eyes and take me into Your kingdom."

When I opened my eyes from my prayer, I spotted what looked to be two ruts that led off the country road. As I let my eyes follow the little road, I could dimly see an old farmhouse. I was encouraged to see smoke rising from its chimney. I immediately started walking, running and stumbling down the road to the house. As I did so, I tripped and fell in a hidden ditch while breaking through the ice. The water was not deep. But, it was enough to get me thoroughly wet. I was now in big trouble as ice began to quickly form on my clothes and a chilling cold penetrated my body.

The closer I got to the house, I could see that it was a relic from the past. It was one of those designs that was built for practical function rather than form. In fact, I realized that it was much like a house my grandmother lived in before her death.

I guess I was starting to get hypothermia, for I started remembering my grandmother's explanation as to how the style evolved. She said the house needed to have a way of ventilating the stifling heat in the hot summers. Therefore, most of the houses had a hall running through the center of the house with high ceilings that allowed the air to move freely through the house and lower the heat index. The kitchen, bedrooms, parlor and other rooms were generally on each side of the central hallway. Windows and screen doors were opened throughout the house in the summer, which allowed the hallway draft to literally suck the air in and out. Along with a wrap-around porch, this arrangement offered an effective way of surviving the sweltering days of summer. On the other-hand, it was a killer in winter as the north wind would find its way through every crack or loose window sash. I remembered when I visited her around Christmas time that it took a lot of firewood to keep her house warm, or at least it seemed like it, because the job fell on me to bring in the firewood.

As families grew smaller and air conditioning became available to the rural areas, most of the old farmhouses were replaced with doublewides or factory built houses. As a result, a piece of American history was bulldozed over, and I hated it. This was a house that had missed the destruction that progress brings and I was almost as thrilled to see an old house like this still standing as I was to know that someone was living in it.

On the way to the house in the remaining light of day, I could see a barn and an old outhouse that had seen better days. Vines were smothering the old outhouse and were also making their way to the barn. I could see that this was no longer a working farm, but a remembrance of a past era.

As I approached the steps to the front porch of the old house, I became reluctant to knock on the door and put myself at risk to whoever might answer. I had heard about some of these backwoods people, and I wasn't looking forward to the possibility of a double barrel shotgun looking me in the face. Most of these country people were simply poor and ignorant but good at heart, and would be glad to help a person in distress. However, some of the meanest and most paranoid people that I had ever heard of shared the same land. I didn't know which one I would be facing but there was no going back. I would die if I didn't get out of the cold.

"Hello in the house," I called out hoping that a call would be less surprising than a knock on the door. But the noise of the wind drowned my voice and I couldn't be heard. There was no other choice but to knock on the door. I stepped onto the porch and knocked. After a brief wait the sound of steps on wooden floors were heard as the resident of the house made his way to the door. The door slowly opened. I waited nervously as I wrapped my arms around my shivering body and tried to keep warm the best I could.

"My, oh my, who is this calling me out in this weather?" a voice cheerfully exclaimed from inside the house as the door opened. I couldn't see the body with the voice because of the darkness, but the tension that was building up in me relaxed as I realized that its owner would be one of the good guys I was hoping for.

Light switches were flipped on lighting the porch and the hallway inside the house. The screen door slowly moved as I eased back from the door so that it could open. When the door opened, the smiling face of an elderly man of African decent greeted me. The first view of the man showed a full set of gleaming teeth highlighted by snow-white hair. I felt immediate relief and comfort that I was welcome in this man's home.

"Mister," I started to say, "I've run off the road with my truck and...." But, before I could complete my sentence, the resident interrupts, "Son, come in this house and get warm. You're going to get mighty sick if we don't get you some dry clothes. Let's go to the kitchen and let you get warm by Old Bessie while I get you some more clothes to put on."

Before I could resist, the old man took me by my arm and led me into the house, down the hallway and into the kitchen. When I entered the kitchen I started to wonder if I had entered a time warp and had been transported 100 years to the past. The only "modern" convenience that was evident was a single light bulb suspended from the ceiling by a dangling wire and an old refrigerator with its motor perched on the top. I had seen pictures of these old refrigerators, but I had never seen any up close. In the center of the kitchen was the biggest wood stove that I had ever seen. Black cast iron with white enamel doors and lifted off the floor with nickel plated cast iron feet, this, I assessed, must be "Old Bessie." From the kitchen door I could feel the radiant heat from the old stove.

The old man pulled a chair from under a small kitchen table and brought it near the stove. Next he took a metal cup from an old pie safe and poured steaming hot coffee into it from an enameled percolator that had been warming on the stovetop. He handed it to me, with a smile.

"You sit here, son, and I'll be right back. There's cream in the fridge and sugar on the table if you want to doctor the coffee up," the old man said as he walked out the door.

I sat next to the old stove and warmed. The coffee helped to take away the chill. I didn't exactly know how to process the last few minutes, for I had never seen anyone like the old man. I had never met anyone that was so willing to give such hospitality and help to a perfect stranger.

I thought, "Surely, like most people, he would have to be wary of just anyone that knocked at his door. To bring someone in his house like this could be dangerous, and at least inconvenient."

I knew that if given the same opportunity as the old man, I wouldn't even had come to the door, much less invited someone in. I was only glad that I wasn't dealing with someone like myself when I knocked on his door.

I continued to study the kitchen. Even though it was old, it was thoroughly clean and in remarkable condition. There was no sink or running water, but instead, a hand pump and washtubs of different sizes that were on a table next to the pump. A large cabinet with a flower sifter, the pie safe holding the enamel cups and dishes, a kitchen table with chairs, and the refrigerator, along with "Old Bessie," made up the kitchen. I also noticed that the old man must have been cooking his supper, for there were several items that were on the table ready to be prepared.

I heard the old man walking down the hallway. Before entering the door he began to speak. "Son, you put these clothes on while I get a fire started in the other room." Before I could say anything the old man handed me the clothes and turned back in the direction he came from.

I looked at the clothes. They were old but clean and had the smell that only sun drying can give. Again, a pleasant memory of long ago invaded the moment as I remembered my grandmother. A flannel shirt, sweater, jeans and thick socks completed the wardrobe given to me. I stood and stripped the wet pants, shirt and socks off. I put the old man's clothes on and quickly discovered that they were made for a much bigger man than me, but, oh how good they felt!

I didn't know what to do with the wet clothes, so I draped them on a chair in the corner of the room. I then sat back down to warm by the stove and to drink the delicious coffee.

As I was drinking my coffee, I picked up another familiar smell as the old man started a fire in the fireplace in the room next to the kitchen. It had been a long time since I had smelled a fire being started with pine kindling. Most modern fireplaces have gas starters or gas logs and the use of "pine lighter" is almost history. There is no hotter or better starter to use to get oak wood roaring than pine kindling. It also gives off a distinct resin smell as it burns. It is this smell that continued to remind me of my childhood.

The normal reflexes that had kept my emotions on guard began to relax and I slowly unwound from a day fraught with strain and tension. I was tempted to nod off, but before I could, the old man returned, poured himself a cup of coffee, pulled up a chair and sat across from me.

He then reached out to shake my hand while stating, "My name is Gabe. Are you warm and dry?" I nodded that I was and introduced myself.

"Okay," Gabe asked intently, "now what was that you were saying about running off the road?"

I recounted my trip. I could tell that Gabe was interested as he grabbed hold of every word. I then asked if there was a motel or town nearby so I could get help and find a place to spend the night.

Gabe answered, "There's a small town about 20 miles down the road and they have a wrecker service, but no one will be getting out in this weather. I don't have a telephone but when the storm stops I'll get out my truck and take you there. As far as a place to stay, you're welcome to stay here. Besides, there is no way we should get out in this storm tonight."

I thought about the offer and said, "I would hate to impose on your hospitality, but it appears that I don't have a choice. I'll be glad to pay you for your accommodations and inconvenience."

Gabe stood, walked to the stove and poured another cup of coffee as he shook his head. "Son, I guess you haven't come to understand the joy someone can have by just being a blessing to someone in need. You've probably been living in such a dog-eat-dog world that to give a helping hand to someone in trouble is a sign of weakness or worse, you don't help for you think he brought it on himself. Now don't you worry about paying me for my inconvenience because I've been well paid for these services way before you ever walked in my door. You're my guest and it is my pleasure to help you. Now I've got an idea that you haven't had anything to eat for a while and could use some supper, am I right?"

71

I hadn't thought about it but I was beginning to feel weak from not eating all day. When Gabe mentioned it, I realized that something to eat would be good.

"Gabe," I answered, "that would be really good. Is there anything I can do to help?"

Gabe waived off the offer for help and told me to get warm and to enjoy being out of the cold.

I watched Gabe move quickly and efficiently through the kitchen as he prepared supper for the two of us. I could tell that Gabe was skilled and well practiced in his cooking. Before long the aroma of fried chicken and biscuits in the oven filled the kitchen. Several pots on the stove stewed various vegetables. I couldn't wait for the meal.

I enjoyed watching Gabe work on the old wood stove. It was a real art to open and close the stove's vents in order to control the heat on the cooking surfaces and the oven. Gabe was a master at it. Before long he pronounced that supper was ready and for me to "Get washed up," as he pointed to a washbasin next to the pump. As I washed my hands, Gabe prepared the table with the food and waited for me to sit down.

When we sat down at the table, Gabe reached for my hand and closed his eyes. Without any announcement he let out a long sigh and prayed softly and intimately.

"Jesus, Lord. You are so good to me. I can never thank You enough for Your blessings in my life. For that reason I am grateful that You have given me an opportunity to thank You by serving this young man. Let me give to Him what You give to me. Most of all let Him see You as You really are and come to know You like You really want to be known. He has been on a long, dangerous journey, but You have kept him safe. Show him Your plan and purpose for his life as You open his heart to Your wisdom. Thank You for this bountiful harvest we are about to eat. In Your name I pray. Amen."

I was taken back by Gabe's comfortable and intimate conversation with the Lord. The prayer was simple but profound to me. I was amazed that Gabe had asked that my heart be opened to God's wisdom as I remembered the voice early that morning telling me to "listen with my heart and not my mind." This was just too profound to be coincidental. In my inner being I was starting to realize that the sovereignty of God was at work with the events that had led me to this man's table. I realized that Gabe knew something about God that I needed to know.

The meal was even better than I had hoped for. Every bite of chicken and mouth full of vegetables lingered with flavor. The hot biscuits, butter and homemade fig preserves complemented the main course. I caught myself rushing to the next bite so quickly that I appeared to be famished. I had to purposely slow down and converse with Gabe, while all along I couldn't wait for the next bite. There was plenty to eat but thanks to me, there was little left over. I could see that Gabe enjoyed watching me wolf down the meal as I caught him smiling from the involuntary "hmmm" I made after each bite. I have eaten some wonderful meals in my lifetime, but never had I ever eaten a meal that was so satisfying as the one Gabe provided me that night.

After our dinner, Gabe allowed me to help with the dishes. He also allowed me to bring in firewood that had been stacked on the porch and to feed the fires that were warming the old house. For the most part Gabe wanted to serve me and to make sure I was comfortable. Since the storm was still raging and I was strongly aware that had it not been for Gabe's hospitality I would have been in a desperate situation, I was most happy to be with Him that night. But more than my circumstance that delivered me to his house, was the joy I was discovering as I was getting to know the old man. I had never met someone who exuded so much joy and zest for life. It was becoming contagious. The more I was around him, the more I wanted to see life through his eyes.

After dinner we continued to linger around "Old Bessie" until late into the night. Our conversation remained relaxed but little-by-little, it started to move deeper as privacy walls were voluntarily let down. For the most part, I felt comfortable sharing with Gabe my background and some challenges that I had faced in life. He seemed to deeply empathize with me when I shared the tragedy of losing my parents in a car wreck a few years back. He was also enjoyed hearing my stories about my grandmother and her house since it reminded me of his. I told him how I used to watch her cook on her old wood stove and how I realized it was a lost art. He laughed as he said he never considered himself an artist. Never had I felt so relaxed in sharing this part of my life as Gabe gave ear to years of layered-over memories.

It was about this time that I received a call on my cell phone. I noticed that I was now getting a faint signal, but realized it wouldn't last long. It was my wife. Briefly I recounted the day and my stranding. She said that the storm was predicted to last for two days. So it appeared that I would be remaining with Gabe longer than initially expected. Before the signal faded out we said that we would touch base the next day, if possible. She was relieved that I was safe and warm. She said that the children were excited about staying home from school, and then the signal was lost completely. Even though cut off prematurely from our conversation, I felt that a small burden had been lifted by talking to her and making sure that all was well. This was the last thing that allowed me to finally relax before the fire and to enjoy Gabe's companionship.

As I finished my conversation on the cell phone, Gabe was extending to me a glass of milk and a slice of apple pie fresh from the stove. I was well treated and well nourished as the finish to a wonderful meal was concluded with the pie and milk. I was also being ministered to in a way that had no words attached, but with simple kindness and sincere joy in giving. I felt as if I was being allowed to have a front row seat to see a man worship his God by the way he was treating the stranger who had invaded his life. It was apparent that there was no hypocrisy in this man. The acts of kindness being conveyed to me were between this man and his Lord. He was not showing off, trying to prove anything or making a point. It was pure worship and I was privileged to see it. I realized that I had much to learn from this man and I was glad to have an extended time with him.

Gabe looked at me intently and observed, "You are a weary traveler. Why don't you go to bed and get a good night's sleep. It appears that we will have plenty of time tomorrow to get to know each other. With that he stood and pointed to the room he had prepared for me.

I must admit I had not had a lot of time to soak in the appointments of the house. The smells of food and the fires in the fireplace had captivated me early on. I was now being ushered to the room I would spend the night in.

Upon entering the room I immediately noticed that Gabe had a roaring fire going in the room's fireplace. Against the wall stood a 4-post iron bed. The bed was draped with a patchwork quilt and cotton pajamas lay across the bed. The house had heart-pine floors throughout. As a result, a warm, golden hue emanated from the fireplace and the surrounding room. As I looked at the room that was prepared for me, I was overwhelmed with gratitude for this man's love for our Savior and the way he expressed it in the way he served me.

"Gabe," I began, "I don't know how I could ever thank you for your hospitality and your gift of this night to me. I have much to learn from you and what you know about our King."

"I think you and I have been brought on a path that we will journey together on, at least for a while" Gabe replied. "Let's see where that might lead. In the mean time, let's get a good night's sleep."

I could tell that Gabe was tired and was ready to turn in. I bid him good night and closed the door.

I quickly prepared for bed and jumped into it. The feather mattress swallowed me into it. The storm was still raging outside. But I was safe, warm and comfortable. The fire mesmerized me, as the flames danced from the burning wood. I reflected on the day's challenges and the events that had led me to this point.

"Lord, I prayed, "I can see Your hand at work throughout this day. I feel that you are preparing the answer to what it means to abandon myself and to truly trust You. I will listen to Wisdom as it speaks to me. Help me to listen with my heart and not my mind."

As I prayed this prayer, I felt a calm assurance that this was indeed what was happening and that Gabe would be God's messenger to me. With this prayer, I slipped off to sleep.

Chapter 15

Revelation

ABOUT DAWN, I AWOKE with the same words I had heard the morning before. "Wisdom will speak. But you must listen with your heart, not with your mind. Listen to My servant and he will guide you," startled me awake. I'm about as practical as anyone when it concerns dreams. I'm not one to put complete trust in dreams as if they are always a message from God. However, my practicality was being challenged with these early morning wake-up calls and the way the events were falling in place.

As I lay in the warmth of the bed, not really wanting to stir, I could hear the rattling of pans in the kitchen and the smell of coffee brewing. The smell of bacon being fried on Old Bessie hung in the air and invited me to go join Gabe.

I quickly dressed, for the fire in the fireplace had long died out and the cold was taking over the room. I ventured to the kitchen and, as before, saw the old man busily preparing the morning meal for his guest. As I entered the room I pronounced, "Best night's sleep I ever had. You need to open a hotel."

Without looking up Gabe responded with a twinkle in the corner of his eyes, "You couldn't afford me...or worse than that, with the way you eat, I couldn't afford you." We looked at each other after his comment and broke into laughter, for we were both well aware how good his meals tasted to me.

While pouring my coffee I hesitantly ventured a comment. "Gabe, do you put much stock in dreams?" He answered, "Most of the time, no; but lately I've been thinking a little different about dreams. Why? Are you having some new dreams that are different from the others?"

I told him about the last two mornings that I had received the wake-up calls. Gabe looked perplexed as he listened. I asked him what he thought. He responded, "You might want to sit down when you hear that answer." Gabe poured himself a cup of coffee and sat in the chair directly in front of me as I sat down. "The last two mornings I've been awakened with these words:"

"Share what I have taught you and Wisdom will speak. Share what I have taught you and Wisdom will speak," Gabe repeated twice.

Now, about this time I was having a chill move up my spine, but not from the cold. It felt like a current of electricity tingling through my body when Gabe shared his dream. It was apparent to both of us that God had carefully orchestrated events in such a way that we were brought together for a purpose. We were both excited about what would be happening even though we had no idea what it would be.

We quickly finished breakfast. Neither of us was interested in lingering long over the food. We wanted to find some answers and discover what the Lord was leading us to.

Gabe brewed another pot of coffee while I cleaned the dishes. We both brought in some more firewood. It was deathly cold outside, even though the storm had blown through. I thought the house was cold inside until I went outside. It was obvious that the old house did not compare with the energy efficient homes of today. But it did keep the occupant alive, provided the fire was stoked up in the fireplace.

While Gabe was busy wrapping up things in the kitchen, I was feeling the urge to take care of some essential personal duties.

I must say I had been dreading the outhouse experience. It had been a long time since using one of those things. My grandmother eventually replaced hers. But in my younger years I was forced to use it when I visited her. I've seen too many spiders, bugs and other critters living in those places. I was always afraid something would reach out and grab me. The imagination of a child can get pretty vivid sometimes. They also make an adult relive some unresolved nightmares if he has to return to a place he once dreaded. I wondered how I would do when I ventured back to my nightmare.

I didn't say anything to Gabe, but simply eased outside to the old outhouse I had seen when I first walked up to Gabe's house. In the light of day I could see that it was even worse off than when I first saw it. It was vine covered and now almost covered with snow. But I had no choice. I was amazed at Gabe's capacity and that he had not had to go to the outhouse since I had met him. I was feeling empathy for the old man for I could see why he would put it off as long as possible. I could just imagine the inconvenience of having to leave a warm house and make a daily run to the old outhouse.

After wading through the snow to get to the outdoor privy, I had to pry the door open while digging the snow back with my feet. The inside of the outhouse was much like my grandmother's in that it was a "two hole wonder." I didn't want to take long because of the cold and those other reasons creeping back into my memory. So I quickly lowered my pants and sat on the seat. As soon as I sat down, I heard a noise under the seat. It scared me to death, as it brought back memories of hidden demons ready to snatch me into the abyss below me. I jumped up and began to run out of the outhouse, forgetting that my pants were still down. As soon as I cleared the door, I fell face first into the snow. As I looked up, I saw the source of the noise. It was a raccoon. This disturbed animal was as unprepared for my visit as I was for his hasty exit through the other toilet hole. We were both very upset.

I looked around, hoping that Gabe had not seen my crash from the outhouse. To my relief he was nowhere to be seen. Disturbed by my experience, I decided to endure a while longer while I figured out a better plan than using "Hotel Raccoon." I dusted the snow off my face and front, and then went back into the house.

When I entered the house, Gabe was sitting in his chair reading his Bible. Without looking up he said, "You know I just thought of something. You might need to go to the bathroom. If so, I have an inside toilet in the back over there," pointing over his shoulder. "It has indoor plumbing and a little electric heater in it. I got tired of going outside on days like today. So, I had a new one put in. I haven't used the old outhouse outside in ten years. In fact, I think a raccoon has taken it over."

I headed to the hidden bathroom that Gabe had motioned to. Under my breath I said, "Do tell. That would be a good thing to know, Gabe!" I swear I think Gabe was fighting back laughter as he was biting his lower lip. That ole rascal probably saw the whole thing. When I settled down, I couldn't help laughing myself. What a sight it must have been.

When I returned, Gabe and I settled into the comfortable chairs that faced the living room fireplace. Since Old Bessie was still hot in the kitchen and a fire was roaring in the living room fireplace, which was adjacent to the kitchen, we were warm and comfortable. Our plan was to spend our day between these two rooms and discover the wisdom the Lord promised.

I started our conversation by saying, "Gabe, I think there is some background that you need to have. I feel that what I am being led to understand is part of a vision God gave to me almost a year ago. I feel that He's taking me to another step that I need to make, but I'm not sure what or how it should be made."

"Why don't you bring me up to speed and tell me as much as you can remember about the vision?" Gabe asked. I settled back in my chair and took a sip of coffee. Gabe did the same.

A quick thought entered my mind that I was so comfortable sharing with this man even though it was obvious there were many differences between the two of us. The un-reconciled differences that permeate our society have created distrust among people that are different, resulting in an inability to relate to one another. I am a middle-age southern white man and Gabe a black man in his 80s. I am a college-educated, middle-class, businessman and Gabe a rural farmer who had very little formal education and little material things. These differences would often make two men deaf or silent to each other. They keep people from considering the values that are shared and even the hope they have in common. Only when someone leads out and breaks the code of silence are things held in common discovered.

Gabe had already led out. He had demonstrated to me that his perspective was not dictated by culture, race differences or the value system of the world. There was something about this man that intrigued me and lured me to him. It invited me into his world and I wanted to go there. Not only did he demonstrate to me an authenticity in his worship of our King, I perceived that he had been given a wisdom that was not of this world.

An epiphany occurred as I realized that this was a foundational truth that God was establishing in me to live by. He was leading me to understand that His wisdom comes from many sources and I should not prejudge His messenger. I couldn't help but be convicted of how much truth and wisdom I had missed in my life because I prejudged people based on their race, age, sex, social status or education. God was speaking to me in that moment about the beauty of His diverse creation and the insight to be gained from a different point of view from my own. Yes, I knew little about this man and my world would tell me to be cautious. Most certainly my world would tell him to be more cautious and not let me into his house or provide me safety or treat me with such generosity and Christian love. But he didn't operate by a code dictated by this world. His code of conduct was out of this world and from another Kingdom. Gabe represented his King and his King's ideals most well.

We both also knew that our paths had been given a divine mandate to cross and Gabe would be an instrument in God's hand for imparting to me the wisdom I was looking for. I didn't know what was in it for Gabe. But I suspected he considered it an opportunity to put hands and feet to his worship of our Savior and that was enough for him. I had a brotherly love growing within me for this new friend as I could see the treasure in God's eyes that he was. I whispered a silent prayer before answering Gabe, "Father, I thank you for this man and for putting him in my life. Help me learn from him."

After my silent prayer, I began to share about the vision. The fact that there was a winter snowstorm blowing outside the farmhouse helped the recall. There was a similar storm the night of the vision.

I wanted to give Gabe as much background as possible, so I spent some time giving him background on my life's struggles before the vision. I told him about my family and the way I had been neglecting them. I told him about my struggles with uncontrollable habits that I kept secret from the view of my friends and loved ones. I told him of my hypocrisy as a Christian and how I struggled with guilt. I knew that he understood the state of my life before the vision because of the concern I saw on his face. He knew the danger my family and I were in.

After the background was established, I then talked about the vision of following Messenger through the Refugee Camp, across the Bridge, to the Banquet Table and to the door to the Inner Chamber. I told him of the impact the vision had made on my life and the changes that had occurred afterwards. I could see the relief and delight in his face with this news. When I explained to him how a group of men was traveling with me on a "sacred journey" to intimacy with Christ, tears formed in his eyes. When I revealed to him our efforts in becoming self-feeders on God's Word, he confirmed that he knew this important secret by the twinkle in his eyes. All in all, my sharing and answering his questions about the vision took up most of the morning.

It was time for a break, for the several cups of coffee that we had enjoyed demanded relief. I had been ready for it for a while. But I waited for Gabe's suggestion. Finally he said, "Let's take a bathroom break. It's your choice. You can use the indoor or the outdoor toilet. However, ole Randy Raccoon out there might not like you invading his home."

With that I replied, "You old rascal, you saw the whole thing and let me go out there this morning! You knew what would happen!"

Gabe was walking away and called over his shoulder, "Haven't got a clue what you're talking about." But he was grinning from ear to ear.

Chapter 16

Wisdom Speaks

ALTHOUGH I WAS STILL SATISFIED by the great breakfast, Gabe suggested a piece of the apple pie and a glass of milk for a snack lunch. While he was working on that project, I brought in a load of firewood and fed Ole Bessie and the fireplace. The storm was not letting up and it was even colder than early morning. I shook my head and uttered a prayer of thanksgiving for not having to be out in the cold. It would have been death for me had I not found Gabe and his house.

When we returned to our chairs, Gabe was the first to speak. "Do you understand the truth about true intimacy with Christ and how it expresses itself to the world?" Without my answer, Gabe continued, "There is a dynamic expression that results when a child of the Living God is dwelling or abiding in that relationship. It is called "fruit" in the Bible. But it is beyond our understanding as to how it works and how far reaching it is. We only know that there is a supernatural occurrence in our life and in the lives with whom we come in contact. It gets picked up without words or our natural senses. We just know that there is something different with the person and we want to share in it. It does liken to being thirsty and wanting a drink of water. Jesus called Himself 'Living Water.' When a child of God is abiding with this 'Living Water,' Jesus is supernaturally sensed in that person. This person becomes a conduit for that 'Living Water' to pass through his or her life to another person. Do you understand this process?"

I thought of when I first met Gabe how impressed I had been by his demeanor and how it drew me to him even though I knew little about him. I could understand now by this explanation that what I had seen or sensed was the "Living Water" Gabe was talking about. It was Jesus within Gabe bearing witness of the truth that Gabe was living in an abiding relationship with the Lord. It was Jesus within Gabe reaching out to me and loving me through this man. This helped me understand how we share Jesus with others. It is not only our telling about Him, it is actually our sharing Him with others. We share His life in us with others. We share the "feast" of what He means to us and for us with others. Somehow the great impossibility of loving the unlovable person now seemed possible. I can't convey grace; only God can. But I can let Him convey it through me. Him in me doing the impossible became another foundation principle that I felt God wanted me to establish.

Gabe continued, "Do you understand the truth of God's Word, and how His Word leads us to this intimacy with Him? From Genesis to Revelations, the theme is consistent. Our God is an intimate, loving and caring God that wants to have an ongoing, intimate relationship with His children. With the sacrifice required by Him and offered by Jesus, the doors of Heaven have been thrown wide open to us. The Holy of Holies that we read about in the temple represent His presence. The temple veil that surrounded the Holy of Holies represented separation. This veil was ripped from top to bottom when Jesus was crucified and thus paid the price that our sins required. This ripping of the veil was a symbolic sign from God that we are invited into His presence and into His arms. Through Jesus we are welcome. The problem is most Christians have gladly received their redemption but have not ventured deeply into this intimate relationship that our King is inviting us to. They remain just inside the veil and try to keep hold of their world with an iron grip, rather than finding the peace and power that is found beyond the veil. For this reason, they are in conflict and do not come into the peace that God wants to give them."

"Why do we do this Gabe?" I asked.

"We cannot grasp the truth and completeness of grace," Gabe answered without hesitation. "Our understanding of grace seems to be limited to our salvation alone. We don't realize that it also delivers us into our Savior's arms along with His Kingdom."

"In your vision you were led across the Bridge, which represents Jesus, and into the Castle, which represents the Kingdom of God. True Believers understand that it is only through Jesus that we are saved. It is only through Him that we can come into God's family. Most Christians understand this and accept it readily. Now this is where God's children get cloudy in their understanding of what more has been done for them. Your vision pointed this out. Within the Castle you were taken to the Inner Chamber which represents relational intimacy with our Savior. You were shown that there is more than Christian affiliation that is given to us. You were shown that there is still more to enjoy and to experience with our Living God. You were also shown that there are some requirements of you to enter this level of intimacy with the King."

Gabe's explanation opened my eyes to things I had not ever considered before. A picture of the inscription on the Inner Chamber doorpost flashed into my thoughts, "He Who Enters This Chamber Must Do So By Personal Abandonment and Absolute Trust."

As I was contemplating the thought, Gabe said, "You said you were initially frightened when you saw the level of commitment required of you in order to enter this deeper intimacy. Why were you frightened?"

I answered, "The thought of abandoning all of my rights to myself and trusting God absolutely with what, how and when He would use me, scared me to death."

"But you were comforted by Messenger, were you not? What did he say to you?"

I answered Gabe, "He asked me if I had forgotten my current spiritual condition? He also asked me if I understood better that God's Word instills courage and that is why I needed to be a self-feeder and grow stronger through it."

"How are you on the 'self-feeding' aspect of your spiritual journey?" Gabe asked.

"This past year I've made it a daily habit to get time in God's Word. It was hard at first but it has become easier, and even necessary, for me as I have been getting a lot of joy from His promises and His assurances. Funny thing, it seems that I have grown in confidence and understanding of things that were vague to me before this practice," I asserted.

"What else did Messenger say to you when you were outside the Inner Chamber?" Gabe inquired.

I answered, "He said that my fear revealed that I was not yet ready to enter the Inner Chamber. He said that when I grow spiritually as a result of feeding on God's Word, my experiences with trials, relying on His promises to get me through them, and His peace that comes when He fulfills the promises, my confidence in the fact that He will always help me would grow. He said that God's faithfulness would eventually override my fear. He said that I would then be ready to enter through the doors and into the Feast in the Inner Chamber."

"Have you had some trials this past year that God has used to show His faithfulness to you?"

I thought of some things that had happened within our family and my job the past year. In fact, there was a point that I was a little discouraged and thought that maybe my new commitment was creating more problems than ever before. However, each time there was a test, I prayed and asked for God's help. Sure enough, He would provide an answer or a solution or a remedy. Every time something would come up, He would provide a way for us. I have to admit after a year of this, I had less fear about how things would turn out. I also had more joy after I saw Him come through for us. I felt closer to Him after every test and more confident in His faithfulness. Gabe had helped me understand more clearly Messenger's words.

"What about the latest test that you experienced yesterday?" Gabe asked. "Can you relate it somehow to God's plan to bless you and prepare you to take that step into the Inner Chamber?"

"Man, did it?" I thought, as I quickly remembered the desperate moments when I was facing the possibility of freezing to death. Since our conversation was relaxed, I didn't feel compelled to answer Gabe directly. I had the social freedom to allow my mind to drift away from our conversation and to think through Gabe's question more deeply.

I thought of my prayer inside the tent before the storm erupted. I remembered it word for word. "Father, I'm here to listen to You. I feel Your leadership to trust You more, but I'm not really sure how to do this. I feel Your delight as I have grown closer to You. I want to grow even closer and become the man that You want me to be and the one who can serve You best. I realize that I cannot do it on my own. I need Your hand on me to accomplish this, but I also know that I play a part. I need to know what that part is so that I can do it. Father, lead me this night and these next days to know what steps I need to take next," came to mind.

Then it started to come together. God had been showing me an example through the humble man that sat across from me, what supernaturally happens when a man abides with the King. There is a holy influence that speaks louder than words from his life, and this influence impacts those that come in contact with him. This influence is not limited to a title or lack of it. It is not limited by economic standing. It is not limited by cultural or racial heritage. It is not limited by age or geographical location. In fact, it could sometimes be obscure and hidden away from the mainstream of the world as with Gabe. But through God's sovereign control, the world will find such a person and beat a path to his door to find answers for the hole that lives in their hearts. A hole that can only be filled with the intimacy our Savior wants to fill it with. I could also see clearly that God was showing me that this was the man he wanted to make of me and it was time that I take those frightening steps.

The door to the Inner Chamber came to mind and its inscription. "Was I ready?" came the questions to myself. "Was I ready to abandon all other ways and to trust the Lord totally and exclusively? Did I really know what this would mean?"

"Gabe," I finally responded. "I can see that God has been showing me that He knows me and everything about me, that He cares about me and everything about me, that He is sovereign over all things and that He is wants to be involved in my life in all situations. He has been communicating to me a message that He is faithful and that He will never leave me. He is leading me to understand that I can trust that His grace will be sufficient for anything that I will ever face and that I must take the steps necessary to enter into the Inner Chamber. It is there that I can become the man He wants to make of me."

With this response, Gabe nodded his head with approval and allowed my words to hang in the air for a while. While doing so we both silently understood the reason for the convergence of our life paths. Gabe realized that I had found the answer to his question and the next step God was leading me to take. I realized that I needed a real life example to see in action. In Gabe, I was given that example.

The silence was finally broken when I asked, "Gabe, what did it take for you to walk through that door," knowing that he understood that I was referencing the Inner Chamber.

Chapter 17

Free At Last

MOST OF THE TIME WE HAD SPENT prior to this time had dealt with my life and the vision. I was glad to get a break from that focus and discover more about Gabe. I perceived that this man had a lot of history that would reveal how his character and spirit had been formed. I knew that I could not truly understand the many obstacles that he had faced and had to overcome. I did understand that I wanted to learn from him. I had seen so many Christ-like qualities in him. The first things he revealed to me about himself surprised me.

It seems that Gabe was not always the gracious, kind and generous person that I was seeing. In fact, in his teens Gabe had left home early, the very house that he now lived in, and made his way to Chicago. There he indulged in a lifestyle of depravity. After a short life of moral decadence and wantonness, he found himself hooked on cheap wine and living under a bridge. He kept his habits fed by odd jobs, begging and petty theft. He came to his senses one day when he realized the three square meals the Army provided its troops was a feast compared to the garbage he was living off. So he enlisted in time to make World War II.

Like so many African-Americans during that time, his training was in war but his duties were in the mess hall. It was there that he learned to cook. It looked as if it would be in the kitchen that he would finish his contribution to the war effort, until the night that a German bomb crashed through a building Gabe was near. More than twenty troops were trapped next to the unexploded bomb. It would be an hour before help could come to hopefully deactivate the bomb and save the wounded troops. The choice was given to Gabe to watch and stay safe or dive in at the risk of his life, and help. Gabe dove in.

Gabe was a very strong young man back then and was able to lift the heavy timbers without help and clear the blocked doorway. A fire had broken out as Gabe was trying to free the trapped men. Panic was breaking out as they were evacuating. Many ran for their lives leaving the wounded behind while Gabe remained, stopping their bleeding wounds and carrying them out on his back.

After Gabe removed the last soldier from the rubble, he collapsed from the smoke in his lungs. The bomb squad arrived and defused the bomb, saving a block of homes. Gabe and the wounded troops were rushed to the hospital.

It was in the hospital that Gabe met an Army chaplain that befriended him and was concerned for Gabe's soul. This man was able to touch Gabe's heart with the "Good News" of God's great love for him and God's overwhelming forgiveness of his life of sin. Gabe had heard about Christianity, but he didn't want anything to do with it because it had been many of the churchgoing "Christians" around him growing up who treated him like dirt and a subspecies. When he finally was able to see someone who he could really see Christ in, he wanted to know more about this Person of Jesus. When he was able to learn that Christianity was all about the relationship a believer has with God through Jesus, not a cultural heritage or an affiliation with a church or denomination, he was able to see and understand what was real and what was fake Christianity. He had been turned off by fake Christianity and wanted nothing to do with it. However, when he came in contact with the real thing, he could see what was missing in his life and those who misrepresented the Lord's family. He wanted Jesus in his life. He didn't want religion or group acceptance. He wanted all that God offered through the Lord and it was there in that hospital ward that he knelt beside his bed and asked that Jesus come and live in his life.

For the most part, the transformation for believers after making the decision to invite Christ into their life is subtle. This was not the case with Gabe. Gabe had a keen awareness of Christ living within him from the beginning and made a commitment of a surrendered life early on. Many who knew the wild Gabe saw the difference in the young hellion and remarked that he must be destined for the clergy. However, Gabe didn't feel that this was where he would make a difference that was needed the most. He felt led to go back to his family and reconcile the conflict that had caused him to leave. He knew that there were many hurt feelings he had to repair within his own family. He had to face his own demons of anger and prejudice which lay below his outward veneer. There was no better place to fight and win those battles than where it all began. So Gabe returned home.

On his discharge Gabe, was awarded awards for valor and received a personal letter from his congressman thanking him for his contribution to the war effort. His bravery for saving the lives of over 20 servicemen while risking his own life, earned not only a special recognition by his company commander. He also received a letter from the President of the United States, recognizing his bravery. Gabe went home a decorated hero and with the respect of his comrades in arms. The maturity of Gabe's body and mind impressed his estranged family. They could see his character had been honed by the disciplines of the Army. After a few days, however, they recognized where the real difference came from. Jesus had impacted Gabe's life so much that it was almost if a new person in Gabe's body came back home to live. His family around him became hungry for the feast he was partaking of and little-by-little each brother and sister came to ask Jesus into their life. They were influenced by the difference the Lord had made in their big brother. The mother and father were a little slower to respond. But Gabe was in no hurry. He just kept loving and serving them, and before long they were loved into an introduction to Christ.

After two years of living at home, helping his father run the family farm, Gabe's father died leaving him responsible to lead the family, becoming the "father" of the house. Although still a young man, Gabe responded to this new requirement on him and did what he did which was to pray…serve…pray…and serve. Every younger child finished high school, learned a trade and moved on with their own life, while Gabe remained home to make all this possible.

Gabe was in his early 30s when he married the love of his life. She was 10 years his junior and radiated with the love of Christ. In fact, Gabe always said that this was what attracted him to her first. She gave him four children very quickly in their marriage. His mother had moved in with one of the other siblings, while he remained on the old farm-place and scratched out a living. With a new family, a heavy load of responsibility removed because of maturing siblings, Gabe was able to finally get on with his life and start afresh, but with years of practical experience.

Gabe and I shared for hours as he had my complete attention. In those few hours, he gave me the highpoints of 60 years of his life. From the feast and famine of farming to raising a family dependent on their daddy to provide for them, I was able to see the slow, methodical growth of a man forged in character and faith. There was more to this man than he was ready to reveal. I was content with his pace of delivery although I was looking for how he faced those demons he spoke about. I was able to get a glimpse of how before we turned in for bed.

I asked, "Gabe you spoke of some demons of anger and prejudice that you had to face upon returning home. What kind of demons were you speaking of?" I felt I knew the answer, for I had seen many blacks mistreated when I was a child. I was expecting him to talk about how he was mistreated and how he would face prejudice again upon returning home. I was surprised by his response.

"Prejudice means to prejudge someone based on an ignorant assumption," Gabe responded. "The black people have been prejudged to be a certain way by some whites, because these ignorant whites feel that we all act a certain way. The truth is there are good blacks and there are bad blacks. As with all people, we are all different."

Gabe continued, "Some ignorant blacks prejudge whites to be a certain way, when in fact, there are good whites and bad whites. So prejudice is not just about race differences. It's about ignorance. We can have prejudice against people because they are wealthy or poor, clean or dirty, Baptist or Catholic. Prejudging is not limited to a certain race, against a certain people or only against a certain victim. We are all victims and culprits alike. The demons of anger and prejudice that I had to face were in my own life and were of my own making. I was prejudiced against whites, against Christians and against farmers. The fact was, I was just ignorant in my own way and let the hurts of a few people shape my view of the rest of those people."

I asked, "When did it change for you?"

"When I started to let Christ's love for me overwhelm the hate I received from others," Gabe answered. "I decided that it was far better for me to not let the narrow-minded, evil inspired words of a few people drag me into their world. Instead, I decided to drag them into my world by praying for them and letting God do His work on them."

"Did it change their lives?" I asked.

"On many, I don't know for sure. Only God does. On a few? Yes indeed. Beyond your wildest imagination," came Gabe's earnest reply.

Gabe continued, "If I were to sum it up, I would say that when I left home, I was a slave to my anger and bitterness. I would still be that way unless Jesus had broken the cords that enslaved me. He did break them and He brought me back to the source to prove it. On this little parcel of ground He and I weathered storms, droughts, despair and every kind of challenge, just so I could see that He is the best lover of my life and has me in His sight at all time. He has taught me to be a good daddy because I learned from Him. He taught me to be a good husband, by giving a model, what He had to do to love His bride, the Church. I don't know how many have been touched. But, as for me and my family, we know the difference that He has made."

I asked Gabe about his wife and found out that she has died 10 years before. Their four children had all earned college degrees, with one becoming a doctor and another a lawyer. One other child was a schoolteacher and the other a stay at home mom. He had twelve grandchildren and two great-grandchildren.

It had grown late into the night and we were both ready to go to sleep. The storm had finally died to a whisper, although the snow was so deep it would be a couple of days to dig out of it. We both yawned and bid each other good night as we headed for our room. It had been a full day for Gabe and me, but it was not complete. The next day would prove to be the turning point as I would make my first step into the Inner Chamber.

Chapter 18

First Steps

MY SLEEP WAS NOT AS RESTFUL as it had been the previous night. I wrestled all night with what I felt had to be done. The inscription in the vision, the words of Gabe, the events of the last two days, all seemed to weave a message to me that I had to move forward in my spiritual journey. I sensed that if I did not move forward, I would involuntarily fall backward.

When the light of dawn began to show through the windows, I was glad to get out of bed and dress. Gabe had already lent me some rubber boots to use when I went outside, along with a heavy coat and hat. I felt that I needed to assess my car situation and to walk and pray.

The snow had packed tightly and I did not break through too deeply. I was able to walk down Gabe's drive out to the farm road easy enough. The car was as I had left it. There was some traffic as people were cautiously driving to work and to other places required of them.

"Lord," I prayed, as I walked down the farm road, "I'm beginning to understand Your message to me. I know that I have struggled with the commitment of personal abandonment and absolute trust. However, I also know that You deserve nothing less than this from me and all Your children."

The light of the sun began to break over the trees and I could see the beautiful, snow-filled fields that lay on the farmland better. Birds flew through the air, glad to be past the storm so that they could look for food. A red-tailed hawk circled above me as the fresh light of the sun reflected off his wings. I breathed in a deep breath of cold air and whispered, "What beauty You've created Father."

I was reminded in that moment of the words of Jesus, "Look at the birds. They don't need to plant or harvest or put food in barns because your heavenly Father feeds them. And you are far more valuable to Him than they are."

I breathed out, "Father, You are faithful and You have always been faithful, for that is the way You are. I know that I can trust You in everything I will face. You have shown me that there is nothing that can snatch me from Your care. You are my Shepherd and I am your lamb. I am ready now and I am committing to establish this day as the day that I abandon my rights to myself and entrust this life to You. I do not know what that will mean or where it will carry me, but that is Your concern, not mine. I realize that this doesn't mean a life of leisure or a life without trials. I do believe that those trials will always have purpose and they will work for Your purpose. My King, I want to live in Your presence and become the man, yes, Lord, the champion, that You desire that I become."

When I finished my prayer, I began a slow walk home to Gabe's house. I continued to soak in the sunlight and experience the beauty of the day. I felt peace with my decision to take my first steps through the Inner Chamber door, and that the life that I would be living from this point on would be within that Chamber. I thought about the Apostle Paul's words, "I have been crucified with Christ. I myself no longer live, but Christ lives in me. So I live my life in this earthly body by trusting in the Son of God who loved me and gave Himself for me," and I understood its meaning as never before.

On my return to Gabe's house, he had breakfast ready for us. I shared with him my new commitment and he rejoiced with me. After breakfast he drove me to town to secure a wrecker and to start the process for repairing the car and making my way home. It took another day, but I was finally back home with my family and friends. They were next to hear of my decision and to rejoice with me. Several of my friends have now followed me on my journey into the Inner Chamber which has drawn us closer together than biological brothers.

It has been two years since that day I made my decision on Gabe's farm road, and I have never regretted it. Some of the greatest threats and trials of my life have been faced and faced down as my King has used these trials in my training. I don't see them as random any more. I see them as specific, timely, strategic and purposeful.

Gabe and I continued our friendship as the old man mentored me until his death. He became a surrogate father to me. He helped me see things through a different set of eyes and became a balancing voice for me.

When Gabe passed away, he did so in his sleep. His family allowed me to sit with them in the family pew at the funeral as they knew of my love for Gabe and his love for me.

Gabe was always full of surprises as I would discover that there were many things that he didn't say about himself or others. He was always moving forward in his life and his spiritual journey. One of his favorite sayings was, "The past is ground that I've already walked on before and there's no need to walk on it again. I'm moving forward to the King." I think that was Gabe's way of living his life the way the Apostle Paul lived his when he wrote, "Forgetting the past and looking forward to what lies ahead, I strain to reach the end of the race and receive the prize for which God, through Christ Jesus, is calling us up to heaven."

Some of those surprises about Gabe were revealed at his funeral. I had asked him sometime before if people were changed when he determined to let Christ's love for him overwhelm the hate he received from hateful people.

At the funeral it became evident that his plan had worked.

Chapter 19

Farewell to Gabe

GABE'S CHURCH WAS UNLIKE ANY CONGREGATION that I had ever been in before. If there was ever a model of cross-racial love and harmony within a church, it had to be the one that I attended that day. There was a tapestry of shades of color as these members greeted each other with embraces and joy. It was real and it was right.

It had not always been that way. In fact, the church had once been a congregation that only blacks attended. During the turbulent 60s, it was a target of racial vandalism. It was finally completely burned to the ground and the congregation dispersed. There, it's charred remains lay as an eyesore to the community and a memorial of hate and prejudice until a young white man several years after the burning began to organize its rebuilding.

At first he had no support and was stymied with all his efforts. The blacks were distrustful of him and there were no whites joining his effort. Still the young man worked everyday by himself cleaning off the rubble and getting the site ready for a reconstruction effort. Then one day Gabe showed up and helped the young man. They would work every day together doing what they could. Little-by-little other people of both races began to join in. A tent was raised on the site and the young white man served as the first preacher for the congregation that was returning and the whites that were joining it. Out of the ash and rubble, a congregation of love was joined together and this triggered the reconstruction of the church building. After several years the church had grown so much that new buildings had to be added. The influence of this church was being realized the world over as it became a major birthing center for other churches using its model. Missionaries were raised up, supported and dispatched to all parts of the world. Like I said, it was nothing like I had ever seen before.

I could tell that Gabe was deeply loved by many people and his influence had reached beyond all racial, economic and cultural boundaries. There were governors, senators and dignitaries of all types at the funeral. They sat next to people in overalls and thin cotton dresses without feeling the discomfort of being out of place. The church choir was all in attendance. All seats were taken with many standing on the sidewalls of the church and outside the church building.

The choir sang praise and worship music and prepared our hearts for the worship of Gabe's King. There were some tears, but mainly there was celebration as we were there to celebrate the life of a special man.

After the choir had completed its music and the co-pastor, an articulate young black man, had opened with prayer and with Scripture reading, the white pastor who had begun the church's reconstruction stood and approached the podium.

"Gabriel Amos Brown was a beloved friend to some of us," the pastor began, "but best of all he was a spiritual father or grandfather to most of us in some way. Just look around and you will see a life that has been touched directly or indirectly by Gabe."

"Most of you that are here," he continued, "have never met the man and yet your life has been impacted by him. You came today to this memorial service by special invitation of someone who has impacted your life and who has been impacted by this church. You were simply told that a very special person's life will be honored today and you were asked to set aside your busy schedule and join us in this special time. And join us you did, as this is the largest group that has assembled at one time in and around this church building."

"Possibly it is because of the invitation from that friend or family member to come to this service that you are now being introduced to a spiritual legacy passed down to you. Most likely you did not even know where it came from? Through an amazing network of relationships that have been influenced by one another and have somehow tracked back to the man we honor today, you will find a point of origin that begins with him and makes its way to you. How can this be? How can a humble man who spent most of his life obscure and hidden away within a rural setting, impact people in Washington, in Main, in California, in Germany and England? 'Amazing.' you say? Yes it is. It's amazing grace."

An "Amen" filtered through the audience after the pastor finished his initial words.

He then continued, "You are here today to honor a friend or maybe an unknown man to you. In doing so you will understand how he has impacted your life and how his life will continue to impact you long after his body has been transformed back to the dust that it came from."

"Each of you have your own story as you answer that question silently in your mind and link it back to Gabe. We could spend days, weeks, or even years telling the story of this man's influence as we look at the spiritual family tree that has grown from his life and eventually to you. But we don't have that time and knowing Gabe as I did, he wouldn't want it. In fact he would get so bored, he would walk out of here and go work in his garden."

The congregation laughed, as they could visualize the old man walking out the door.

The pastor continued, "Gabe didn't think much about himself. In fact, he was more concerned with others and encouraging us to get our eyes off ourselves. I'll never forget when he and I were the only ones working in the burned out rubble of the old church and I was complaining that no one would help us, especially some of the white community who I felt should be leading the effort. You know what he said to me when I was feeling sorry for myself?"

"All self-pity is from the Devil. Now are you going to listen to him or to God? Get back to work and let Him deal with their hearts!" And deal with their hearts? You know the rest of that story as you have joined in the mission of this church. As Gabe would say, 'Way to go! Now, keep going!' With this statement another laugh from the congregation broke out.

"There is one story that you need to hear and I feel that it's time that you hear it. Gabe has not told this story to anyone. This will be the first time you hear it. It has been a long time coming."

We were all ready to hear the story that the pastor was talking about, for his build-up was so intriguing he had us all on the edge of our seats.

"Some of you know, or know of, Gabe's laughter and joy. What you may not realize is the source of that joy. Gabe always fixed his eyes on his Lord Jesus and has allowed Him to have his way with him. Gabe would not engage in self-pity or allow anger to pull him down. He told me one time that he saw it as a test if he could remain strong, weather the storm and see what God wanted to make out of it. And was he tested? Some of those tests were just part of his 'growing up phase' as he would say. But some of the tests had a strategic design in the life of another person and that is what I'm leading up to. This is the story of a test that Gabe had to face and how it strategically impacted the life of another person, and another person, and eventually to you."

"Several years ago, when Gabe was in his early 40s, raising a young family and trying to scratch out a living on his farm, he had a particularly good year with his crops. In fact, all the other farmers in the county were amazed by his crop yield, especially because their crops had done so poorly. What they didn't realize was that Gabe had figured out crop rotation and organic fertilization methods on his own, and he knew how to nurture the soil by letting it rest when it needed it and to use different crops to put necessary nutrition back into the ground. He also prayed a lot over his crops which he told me he felt did the most good."

"Now, there was a farmer that lived near Gabe that was as mean and spiteful as they come. He was jealous of Gabe's success. Because of this jealousy this man, in the still of night, started a fire in Gabe's barn and partially burned it. Gabe saw the fire and was able to contain it before it got too big and stopped it before it did too much damage. Now the funny thing about it, the farmer who was trying to burn Gabe's barn down stepped in a hole next to the barn and broke his leg as he was running away from his arson. As he was lying on the ground with this broken leg, Gabe came upon him and realized what had been attempted by the man."

The pastor paused his story and asked us, "Now what would you have done if you had been Gabe?"

I could hear a murmur in the congregation as they whispered what they would do.

"Yea, me too!" the pastor said. "But not Gabe. You see, Gabe wouldn't let the evil actions of another person dictate his actions. He marched to the drumbeat of his King. He felt that the test he was facing was whether or not he would let the voice of Jesus lead him over that voice of his enemy. Gabe followed His King's voice.

Instead of dong what you or I would have done, Gabe made a makeshift splint, hitched up his mule to the wagon and drove the man home. Gabe nor the farmer said anything while they drove home. When Gabe lifted the man's arm over his shoulder to help the farmer off the wagon and into his house the neighbor asked Gabe, 'Why didn't you kill me? I would have killed you!'"

"I don't know what his reply was. Gabe never said. But Gabe continued his act of kindness by bringing vegetables and meat to the farmer and his family while he was healing from his broken leg. That food was all this family had to eat during that period, for all the other neighbors detested this man and had no sympathy for him. Little wonder why."

"Now in the house of that farmer who attempted to burn down Gabe's barn, was a young boy who had been raised in an atmosphere of bitterness, self-pity and hatred. The cancer of this atmosphere had made its mark on the young boy and he grew up as mean as his father, maybe even meaner. He got into trouble all the time as he dealt with the rage and self-pity that lived within him. You probably don't know that it was this young, teenage boy who, with some other friends burned this church down several years ago. He didn't get caught, but the guilt and shame of his actions haunted him until several years later."

The congregation was completely silent as they realized they were hearing something about their church history that they had never heard before. It was obvious that Gabe would be involved somehow in the reconstruction of the life that this pastor was talking about, and we couldn't wait for the next sentence.

"The young man left the county and joined the marines," the preacher continued. "He went to Vietnam. He wasn't prepared for the difficulties he would face and had no foundation to weather it. It broke him and he began to cope, as many of our servicemen did in that era, with alcohol and drugs. Fast forward a few years later."

"After his discharge, he became an aimless drunkard and drug addict as he roamed the streets of Kansas City. His family had left the county after his dad had died. He didn't even know where they had moved. He was totally alone in life—no friends, financially broke, emotionally broken and abandoned."

"He hitchhiked back to the old farm that he had grown up on. It was abandoned, just like the rest of his life. He bought a fifth of whiskey and a gun with two distinct purposes, to anesthetize his pain and fear, and to end his miserable life. It was in that setting God intervened by sending Gabe who happened along that day, and found the young man beside the road with a gun in one hand and an empty whiskey bottle in the other."

The preacher paused as we waited for his next words. "When the young man looked at Gabe, he remembered his childhood and how the big black man had helped his father back home one night when he had broken his leg, and how the man had provided food for the family when his father couldn't work the farm. The young man started to curse Gabe but before he could, he passed out from his drunkenness."

"Gabe brought the drunken man into his home. Gabe's children were all away at college, and they probably don't even know this story about the young visitor coming to their mom and dad's home, do they?" as the preacher looked at Gabe's children. They nodded that they had not heard it before.

The preacher took a drink of water from the glass on the podium to clear his throat and continued. "It was in that setting that Gabe and Katherine, Gabe's beloved wife, ministered to this young man, with the love of Jesus. When the young man was drying out and going through the withdrawal symptoms of the alcohol and drugs, it was Gabe and Katherine that were bathing his head and body with cool water and praying over him. They fed him food that was like manna from heaven. When he grew strong, Gabe took the young man to the fields with him and taught him how to work the fields and began to rehabilitate the dignity of a self-proclaimed loser. Gabe showed this young man Jesus by the way he lived his life before the young man, and he then filled in the pieces with a study of God's Word. Little-by-little the love of this man and woman and the servant leadership that Gabe demonstrated began to pay off. The young man felt the love of a father for the first time in his life, and he wanted what Gabe and Katherine had. He wanted Jesus in his life. It was on a clear night when the stars are at their brightest that this young man knelt in the field behind Gabe's house and gave his life to Jesus."

With this last comment a shout rang out from some one in the congregation and everyone began to applaud the decision of the young man. When the congregation calmed down, the preacher continued.

"There was still work to be done with this young man's rehabilitation, but he now had the King of the Universe in his life and Gabe at his side. He was ready to start a new life and follow the King of Kings anywhere the King would lead. Little did this young man realize that the King would lead him to a little burned down church to build it back up. Little did he realize that he would be the first pastor of that congregation and little did he realize that he would be standing before you this day telling you this story of how God used Gabe to turn my life around. But, it is time that I did."

The congregation was stunned! For the first time they realized that the preacher had been telling them his life story. He was the young man who burned the church down several years before, and he was the one that began its rebuilding process. Someone in the congregation began to sing "Amazing Grace," as every person was wiping tears from their eyes. The whole congregation joined in the song as the young, black, co-pastor went to the preacher and embraced him. They both wept and embraced for several minutes. After the song was finished, the preacher continued.

"I share my story with you, but it is not about me. It is about a humble man who God could do great things through. Gabe was this kind of man. Gabe allowed his life to be at God's disposal, he was on God's agenda and he never complained about it. He trusted God and He walked with him. This is the life we celebrate today, and in doing so we cannot help but learn from this life."

"So what can we learn from this life? What are some principles that we can glean from this humble man of great influence? What can we take home with us and apply to our life? I've been thinking about this and watching that man in action for several years, and here is what I've seen. Maybe you'll want to write these down. Maybe you will want to study these principles, and pray about them and embrace them into your own life? If you do, I believe that they will drastically impact your life and one day you could become a person of great influence like Gabe. You too can build a legacy of faith as your life impacts your world around you. You too could one day have a gathering such as this that tracks their spiritual family tree back to you. I call these principles 'Gabe's Principles of Influence.' Here's what they are:"

Gabe's Principles of Influence

• Be a God Seeker: Make it your greatest personal goal in life to grow in your knowledge of Who the Great I Am is. Understand that this will be a life-long pursuit. Gabe never tired or gave up on wanting to know more about God. Seek a daily enlightenment of Who the King of Kings is, all of your days on this earth.

• Be a God Abider: Make it your daily desire to dwell in the presence of the Almighty God. Don't let anything disrupt this. He is your power, your strength, your source of Living Water. It is in His power that He is able to use your life to be able to do the impossible, such as love like Jesus, forgive like Jesus, turn the other cheek and let God make good out of something bad. Gabe was a man that walked with God. He abided in the shelter of the Almighty. As a result, God could use him to help an enemy home when he tried to burn down his barn, demonstrate to a family in need the forgiveness of Jesus even though it wasn't asked for. This kindness that was generated by a deep, loving, gratitude to his Savior, enabled the man to be an instrument in God's hand to save his enemy's son from murdering himself and to lead the son to a life of service for our King. God can do the impossible through one who abides in Jesus.

• Live it out: Gabe had a simple plan for living out his faith. He had priorities and all that he did flowed through this plan. First, was to love his wife like Christ loved the church and gave Himself for us. Second, was to love his children like the prodigal father loved his son and always opened his arms to them. Third, was to embrace his world around him with a sacred responsibility and to express the love that was given to him by Jesus to those God brought into his life, whether they were bad or good.

As the preacher was instructing us in the "Gabe Principles," I was busy writing them down, for I knew that I needed to share them with the men I meet with. As I did, the funeral celebration continued for a while with many testimonials of people who "just had to share a Gabe story." The atmosphere was relaxed. And no one was in a hurry. After a good while, the celebration of Gabe's funeral came to a close. We didn't want it to end. We wanted to somehow hold onto the man and his memory. But, it finally ended.

Chapter 20

The Journey Continues

REFLECTING ON THE FUNERAL, it was apparent to me that the life of the man would be remembered many years afterwards. And long after his memory has faded from history, will be the impact his life has had on generations of people that follow. His life had been used by God to impact me and I am sure that it will be reproduced through me in years to come.

I drove home after the funeral that day and could not help but revisit the spiritual journey that I had been on since the vision. From the time of the vision, God had carefully orchestrated circumstances, events and people to not only reveal to me what was missing in my own Christian walk, but how to fill that which is missing. He also gave me a model in Gabe of what a life looks when one abides with Jesus. I have come to understand that this is what the world is longing for. It needs models of authenticity. It needs to see the difference Christ makes in a life. Not an explanation from us, but a demonstration of Christ in us. In Gabe they saw nothing spectacular. There was nothing about him that drew attention to himself, but what they did see was real, was pure and was saturated with moral authority. Indeed, Gabe was authentic.

As my mind wandered back and forth from the time I first got to know Gabe until that drive home from the funeral. I imagined the "Great White Throne" in Heaven and when Christ will recognize our works for Him and the way we have lived before our life in Heaven. I knew Gabe well enough to know that he would have had no idea the way his memory was honored at the funeral. I also knew that his greatest surprise will still be ahead for him as the Lord will allow him to see the legacy of faith and the impacted lives that sprang from his love for his Savior and his simple obedience. Although the fruit of this faithfulness was seen by the impacted lives at the funeral, the exponential multiplication of those lives reaching others will still continue until Christ's return. And it will be those lives that will be gathered around Christ and His throne that applaud the faithful warrior Gabe who steps forward to receive his reward from his Savior.

I could not let this thought pass without whispering a question to my Savior if my life could ever be as fruitful as Gabe's? Immediately, I was impressed with the thought, "Only if you make it your life's goal to abide with Me, My child. When you abide, fruit beyond your wildest dreams occur. But best of all, you are fulfilling My purpose for your life, which is all that counts. Don't compare yourself to Gabe. Simply seek me and become all that I can make of you, nothing more, but for sure, nothing less."

Yes, that was the answer I needed for that nagging question to what my life's purpose is and how I can give my best for my King. It is not what we do for our King that remains. It is what is produced from the relationship with our King that bears a fruit that lasts. It should not be my concern to create a legacy of faith. My concern is to simply be faithful, and allow any legacy that follows be the result of my abiding relationship with Christ.

This answer to my heart's prayer seemed to complete the final piece of the puzzle as to how my life would best play its part in carrying out my Savior's "Great Commission." I was now at peace and I knew that I had completely walked through the door to "The Inner Chamber." There would never be a return to my old life, as I envisioned the door to the Inner Chamber closing behind me while I stepped into the warmth of a life secure in Christ. My journey beyond the Chamber door had now truly begun and the life ahead would be lived out moving forward from this point to the depths that the Chamber offered me.

What about you? Where are you in your spiritual journey? You know, it is a journey that we are on? It's a sacred journey that is designed to take us to the Feast in the Inner Chamber and then to our world around us as we become an influence for our King. The "journey" I speak of requires the biggest commitment of your life. In fact, it requires a commitment of your life. As God's child, we have to commit to become self-feeders on God's Word. This will help us grow in our understanding of Him and His heart for His children to come closer to Him. From this "self-feeding" we are prepared for our next commitment, which is to abandon our life to our King and to trust Him absolutely. When this occurs, we walk through the doors of the Inner Chamber.

Let me warn you, if you decide to take this journey it is not for cowards, for it will separate the faint-hearted quickly when the challenges come. But on the process this journey takes us through, we will become God's champions and He will show us how to not only live a life that honors Him, but He will also show us how to live life as He created it to be lived, fully alive with purpose, power and peace.

So, if you are ready for the ride of your life, get prepared to mount up! The King is dispatching us to the marketplace, for there is another Refugee out there whose heart is ready to come back with us to the Kingdom, and we have to show him the way. Come with us. We need help by having more Influencers in the marketplace who will demonstrate the truth about our Savior's love and rescue plan. These are the kind of people who the world is ready to listen to. We can really make a difference. But remember, there is a plan God has given us to follow, if we want to make that difference. To be a true Influencer requires that we be under Christ's influence, and this kind of influence is found only in the Inner Chamber as we learn to abide with Him there.

Epilogue

THERE SHOULD BE A POINT in every believer's life when he evaluates the progress he is making in his spiritual journey. The most accurate measurement comes not in his comparison with other people or his spiritual works, but in the intimacy with Jesus Christ that grows in his life. Why is this? Why would spiritual works not be the best measurement? Let's ask Jesus. In John 15, Jesus teaches His disciples on the necessity of abiding in Him. He said that unless we abide in Him we would not bear fruit (works). He also stated that said it is essential that a believer bear fruit, because this fruit honors Him and it honors the Father.

Here's the point: Jesus said we couldn't bear the kind of fruit He is talking about by our own efforts. We cannot bear fruit that is truly honoring to Him and the Father by willpower, self-help books, or any device man has conceived or created. The fruit Jesus spoke of is of divine origin and comes from our abiding relationship with Him.

'Symbiotic' is a great word to describe abiding in Christ. What does it mean? Webster defines it as: "To live together. The intimate living together of two dissimilar organisms in a mutually beneficial relationship." Dissimilar? How so? For starters, how about the Perfect vs. the imperfect? How about He who can do no wrong vs. he who is bound to do wrong? How about He who is able vs. he who is unable? How about Holy God living with a forgiven, but sinful, man? This is what we have been offered in this magnificent relationship with Christ if we are willing to take it. We are given not only the invitation and the access to God through Christ but also the privilege to dwell with Him like a branch does with the vine. We are invited to a deep, intimate, active, live-in relationship with Jesus. Out of this abiding, dwell-in, symbiotic relationship will be a supernatural reaction. It is called fruit.

How does this fruit occur in the life of the believer? The fruit is not a result of education, title or profession. It is not a result of personal achievement, work ethic or being loved by Jesus more than others are. This fruit is as natural as grapes growing on a healthy grapevine, apples on an apple tree and tomatoes on a tomato plant. When everything is right with the nutrition and climate, the tree or the vine will produce fruit. Likewise, when we abide in fellowship with Jesus in a healthy, unobstructed manner, He will bear fruit through us. When there is a balanced intake of spiritual nutrition along with a healthy spiritual climate, fruit will appear.

What is this fruit Jesus spoke of? Most evangelical Christians would say it is converts to Christ. I would agree that our abiding in Christ would eventually find us joining Him in the fruit of the harvest, but I believe there is a process in our spiritual development that happens before we can be effective fruit bearers in the harvest for the souls of men. I call it the Fruit of Transformation.

What is this Fruit of Transformation? Paul mentions it in Galatians 5:22. "But the fruit of the Spirit is love, joy, peace, patience, kindness, goodness, faithfulness, gentleness, self-control; against such things there is no law." Peter described it in II Peter 1:4 as being "partakers of the divine nature." Another way of describing it is "Christ-likeness."

The fruit of the Spirit describes the nature of Christ. Having the fruit of the Spirit evident in our lives is an indication that He is the One who is in control in this symbiotic relationship. That's our goal, our target. Not that we become better people, although that is a worthy goal. But, rather, that Jesus takes over our life. Our goal is to surrender our nature as a "living sacrifice" so that His nature can take over. When Jesus takes over the controls of our life, there will be fruit and we will eventually join Him in the harvest, as the spiritual gifts that are unique to us are unleashed. When they are unleashed, we will become dangerous warriors for our King.

The story you have just read is an illustration of this spiritual growth. It is a mystical journey that describes the spiritual journey of a particular believer in Christ. This believer is shown the hindrances that kept him from realizing his potential to become the man God wants him to be. He was then shown a path that could take him to that deeper place with Christ, if he was willing to follow it. Perhaps you read your own life story in this book? Perhaps, as a result, you can now identify stops in your own spiritual journey and you now know what action needs to be taken by you to re-start your journey? If this is so be encouraged, for the life of a champion for God can still be ahead for you and you have identified what your next step should be. Know this: Hopefully you desire to be God's champion, then the need for an intentional pursuit of a deeper intimacy with Christ must be your next step. I pray that you are willing to take this step and make your move. We need you to join us in the harvest after you have journeyed to the Inner Chamber and this would be the fruit of your journey to intimacy with Christ.

You will never know what you are missing until you taste the Living Water that is in the Inner Chamber. When you journey there, you will find that which your soul has been thirsting for all your life. It is available and is waiting for you to drink all you desire. But, the next step is up to you. Will you take it?

Rocky Fleming, is a co-founder of Influencers,
a discipleship ministry which equips disciples for
Christ within the business culture. He has retired
from his business as a self-employed businessman in
Northwest Arkansas in order to assist in the development
of Influencers throughout the world, and to
pursue his passion for writing.